the red indians

Copyright ©2007 Peter Kulchyski

ARP BOOKS (Arbeiter Ring Publishing)
201E-121 Osborne Street
Winnipeg, Manitoba
Canada R3L 1Y4
arpbooks.org

Printed in Canada by Kromar Printing Ltd.
Cover by Michael Carroll
Design by Relish New Brand Experience Inc.
Fourth printing, November 2014

ARP acknowledges the financial support of the Government of Canada through the
Canada Book Fund for our publishing activities.

ARP acknowledges the support of the Province of Manitoba through the Book
Publishing Tax Credit and of Manitoba Culture, Heritage, and Tourism through
the Book Publisher Marketing Assistance Program.

We acknowledge the support of the Canada Council for our publishing program.

With the generous support of the Manitoba Arts Council.

LIBRARY AND ARCHIVES CANADA CATALOGUING IN PUBLICATION

Kulchyski, Peter Keith, 1959-
     The red Indians : an episodic, informal collection of tales from the history of
Aboriginal people's struggles in Canada / Peter Kulchyski.

ISBN 978-1-894037-25-9

     1. Indians of North America--Canada--Politics and government. 2. Indians of
North America--Canada--Treaties. 3. Right and left (Political science)--Canada.
4. Indians of North America--Canada--History. 5. Indians of North America--Canada--
Government relations. I. Title.

E78.C2K85 2007   971.004'97   C2007-906111-7

THE RED INDIANS

AN EPISODIC, INFORMAL COLLECTION OF TALES FROM THE HISTORY OF ABORIGINAL PEOPLE'S STRUGGLES IN CANADA

Peter Kulchyski

ARBEITER RING PUBLISHING • WINNIPEG

to the red indians

a long time ago the greek barbarians who ravaged persia under the leadership of alexander reached a river they decided would be the limit of their conquest. local people called that river the 'indus,' so the people who lived beyond it were called 'indians.' the word continued to be a part of european geography long after alexander's time. it covered any of the far eastern peoples known to europeans only through rumours carried along ancient trading trails. centuries later, in 1492, when christopher columbus found land across the ocean to the west of europe, he used the same word to describe the people he met: 'los indios.' from then on, a small confusion of terms circled the colonial conquest of the americas. 'indians' was a term that described widely different people in asia and in the americas.

in the 1980s, apparently, there was a first major attempt by the canadian government to statistically count aboriginal people with the census, using a technique called 'self identification.' they asked people 'are you an indian?' lots of people born in mumbai, amritsar, delhi, kolkata, or other parts of the indian subcontinent replied, honestly, 'yes.' so the data was, as the bureaucrats gently put it, 'skewed.' a word – 'indian' – that had once served colonial power became, finally, too blunt an instrument and had to be replaced.

this book is called *the red indians*, a title that may upset or even offend some people. in calling it that, i am taking an old expression that was used to distinguish north american 'indians' from east 'indians' and giving it a new twist. for me, the red indians are aboriginal leaders who were 'reds,' that is, on the left of the political spectrum. the red indians, leaders like fred loft or malcolm norris, were those who, in fighting for aboriginal rights, saw an affinity or similarity with the struggle against capitalism in canada. they were ahead of their time in recognizing that the values of socialists and the traditional values of aboriginal peoples had much in common. there are no buildings named after fred loft, no monuments to honour most of the red indians. their struggles live in the memories of their descendents and in the gains they achieved for their peoples, which is all they would have wanted. i honour them here. i honour them now. i hope a part of their spirit lives on to inspire a new generation of red indians. and i hope you find some value in these words.

you may have noticed that i do not write with capital letters. i like to borrow from the writing strategies used by modernist writers and poets. i also want these words to look different from the words of other histories of canada, and by not using capital letters i accomplish this: showing in the physical look of these words that history needs to be rethought. also, by not using any capital letters, i avoid the tricky problems regarding which words should be capitalized – indian? aboriginal? indigenous? elder? drum? – that sometimes plague native studies. it is my modest hope that my resistance to capitals parallels or marks my resistence to capital itself.

these stories were originally written as part of a newspaper column i once wrote for the *native press* of yellowknife, under the editorial oversight of lee selleck. in retelling some of them here, i do not pretend to offer a full account of the history of the indigenous peoples of canada. instead, i'm offering a few scattered stories or episodes that may be of interest to you. these stories show how there has been a 'turn to the political' in the last hundred years of indigenous canadian history; that treaties are not a sideline but, rather, at the very heart of canada's constitutional fabric; and that the history of indigenous peoples in canada is the history of canada itself and continues to be the history of canada.

true discoverers and false discoverers
(gasp! are we allowed to use any of these categories?)

in the decade and a half since 1992, there has been a lot of talk about the early european 'explorers,' but, obviously, columbus and jacques cartier and samuel de champlain and samuel hearne and alexander mackenzie and all the rest we hear so much about never actually 'discovered' anything at all. all the land they saw, the rivers and lakes and mountains they gave new names to were already well known, used, occupied, and named by native peoples. to say they 'discovered' all this land is to act as if native people didn't exist and hadn't, for thousands of years, themselves explored and discovered what today we call the americas.

so if we want to celebrate the 'discoveries' of this or that part of america, we should look back, not 500 but over 12,000 years, back to a time beyond recorded memory. we should celebrate the many unknown, everyday native women and men who walked or paddled down new paths, new rivers, who found and invented new ways to live in new lands. we should celebrate how they managed to care for the lands they found, care for those lands so well that years later, european men would mistakenly think the land was pristine, untouched. a humanism that celebrated the achievements of humans, rather than european men, would be willing to recognize and celebrate such an achievement. such a humanism would even deserve its name!

most academic books refer to those forgotten 12,000 years as 'pre-history,' as if only europeans are allowed to make history. but in the centuries before columbus, people lived and died, cultures grew and changed, wars were fought and peace negotiated in the americas. in fact, the last 500 years have not been the best ones for native people. they have been 500 years of disease, warfare, and outside interference in their ways of life; 500 years of conquest and colonialism. but this book focuses on the struggle and resistance in those 500 years. in order to show how indians have in many instances worked with europeans but, increasingly more frequently, had to struggle against them, i will give some broad outlines of historical periods, provide stories of aboriginal individuals, look at some of the important treaties and legal issues, and tell of some crucial moments of aboriginal action in the face of injustice.

sometime in the early morning of october 12, 1492, a member of columbus's crew sighted land. when columbus woke up that morning, what he believed all his life was india lay before him. in peterborough, where i worked in 1992, we decided to celebrate october 11, the day before columbus day, because it commemorates the last day of freedom for the original 'discoverers' and occupants of this land.

from october 12 onwards, freedom for native peoples slowly disappeared. my favourite work dealing with early contact history is eduardo galeano's *memories of fire* trilogy. the first volume, *genesis,* and the second, *faces and masks,* deal with early history of contact focusing on the spanish conquest. i'm obliged to warn you that unlike much of what i recommend, you have to be very, very careful when you read galeano. his words burn.

history is carried by bodies: thanadelthur

biography tells us a lot about how people make history and how history makes people. life histories are a very big part of both native oral traditions and the writings of native people, so, as well as the overall story, let's look at the lives of some of the people who lived it. thanadelthur was a chipewyan woman who lived around the turn of the seventeenth century (late 1600s, early 1700s). we don't know a lot about her life and we aren't even really sure that thanalelthur was her real name; in an account of chipewyan oral history written by edward s. curtis, she was refered to by that name, which he says means 'marten shake'; dene elders from lac brochet in northern manitoba today know her story.

thanadelthur is important historically because she helped bring peace between the cree and chipewyan. apparently, she had been captured by the cree and held for some time by them, possibly as a slave. the cree in those years had access to guns and other european goods, because the hudson's bay company had built a fort in their territory. this meant the cree became key traders, preventing other nations from having contact with the english in order to control the supply of european goods.

in november of 1714, according to the post journals of governor james knight, thanadelthur, having escaped from the cree, made it to fort york. governor knight immediately saw her value, writing "she will be of great service to me in my intention." knight's journal is one of the main sources of information about thanadelthur, whom he always refered to as "the slave woman." his intention was to have thanadelthur go to convince the chipewyan to trade directly with the english.

in the summer of 1715, thanadelthur left fort york with a party of cree indians and an englishman, william stewart. as they got closer to chipewyan territory, the cree grew more and more afraid. so did stewart. only thanadelthur wanted to press on.

finally, when stewart would go no further, thanadelthur told him and the cree to wait for her and she went on alone. after ten days she returned to stewart's camp with "about 160 men" and, as knight wrote, she "had made herself so hoarse with her perpetual talking to her country men in persuading them to come with her that she could hardly speak." she managed to convince the chipewyan not to hurt the cree, probably because she knew that was the only way they would be able to trade directly with the english.

in may of 1716, thanadelthur returned to fort york with ten chipewyan, thus starting direct trade between her people and the english. governor knight said she had been "the chief instrument" in negotiating the peace between the two first nations. in february of 1717 she died of an illness.

translator, negotiator, peacemaker: thanadelthur deserves a place in canadian history. sylvia van kirk has an article about her in the magazine *the beaver.*

reflection of an image of a mirror...

one of the most interesting aspects of the early encounters between europeans and aboriginal americans were the ideas that europeans had about the people they met. from very early on, distorted and incorrect notions about aboriginal cultures played an important role in justifying european conquest.

the two images that became most prominent were quite different from each other. to some europeans, indians were peaceful, at one with nature, gentle and generous. for example, columbus wrote of the people he met: "they are very marvellously timorous … they are so guileless and generous with all that they possess, that no one would believe it who has not seen it. they refuse nothing that they possess, if it be asked of them." amerigo vespucci, writing a decade later, described indians as "a race i say gentle and amenable … in their gait and when playing their games they are agile and dignified. they are comely, too." at the same time, indians were described as ruthless, bloodthirsty savages, often by the same people. for example, columbus described a people he called 'caribs' as "very fierce and who eat human flesh."

vespucci went further, writing, "the nations wage war upon one another without art or order. the elders by means of certain harangues of theirs bend the youths to their will and inflame them to wars in which they cruelly kill one another, and those whom they bring home captives from war they preserve, not to spare their lives, but that they may be slain for food; for they eat one another, the victors the vanquished, and among other kinds of meat human flesh is a common article of diet with them."

these kinds of gross distortions were quite common in the early european descriptions of american indians and inuit. often they stressed aspects of european society that did not seem to be present in aboriginal cultures. amerindians were described by vespucci and others as having no law, no religion, and no government. their cultures were so different from european cultures that, for the europeans, they represented a kind of anarchy.

many historians have noted the presence of these two broad patterns of images of indians: on the one hand as 'good,' so-called noble savages; and, on the other hand, as 'bad,' ferocious savages. the tendency has been to say that these are both wrong and are equally distorted ideas. two interesting books about images of indians are robert f. berkhofer jr.'s *the white man's indian* and tzvetan todorov's *the conquest of america.* a canadian account of the issue can be found in daniel francis's *the imaginary indian* and in olive dickason's *the myth of the savage.*

my own view is that these different ideas mirror or reflect important differences within european society. in order to show why i think this is so, let's take a look at a famous debate that took place in spain in the 1500s over the souls of indians. what is clear is that both these ideas remained influential for a long time and that they appeared at the time of the early encounters.

valladolid and the soul of north america

in april of 1550, at the height of the so-called 'age of discovery,' when countless numbers of amerindians were paying with their lives the costs of this 'discovery,' king charles v of spain, perhaps the most powerful man in europe at the time, asked a very important but simple question.

more importantly, he also ordered all conquests in the new world halted until this question could be answered. the question he asked was: "is it lawful for the king of spain to wage war on the indians, *before* preaching the faith to them, in order to subject them to his rule so that afterwards they may be more easily instructed in the faith?"

two intellectuals were given the task of debating the question. arguing that 'yes,' it was lawful to wage war first and and convert later, was juan gines de sepulveda, a respected court historian and humanist scholar. sepulveda was a well-known academic who had made his intellectual mark with a latin translation of the ancient greek philosopher, aristotle's, book, *politics*. sepulveda's arguments came from books he thought were authoritative. these included the bible, a short text written by the pope called *sublimus deus,* and aristotle. for descriptions of indians, he relied on the writings of fernandez oviedo, a conquistador who had been to the so called 'new world.' sepulveda had never been to america.

sepulveda argued that indians oppressed and killed innocent people and committed crimes against nature. he went so far as to say that "in prudence, talent, virtue and humanity [indians] are as inferior to the spanish as children to adults, women to men, as the wild and cruel to the most meek, as the prodigiously intemperate to the continent and temperate, that i have almost said, as monkeys to men." he basically argued that indians were barbarians and therefore it was lawful (and necessary) to use war in order to prepare indians to receive the christian faith.

arguing the 'no' side was a dominican monk, bartolome de las casas. las casas had spent fifty years in central america. he had started off as a typical conquistador, with slaves of his own, but soon grew disgusted with the treatment of indians. as bishop of southern mexico, he had incurred intense anger from the conquistadors because he refused to allow them to be buried on sanctified ground unless they set their indian slaves free. las casas thought that indians were basically good. he argued that "god created these simple people without evil and without guile. they are the most obedient and faithful to their natural lords and to the christians whom they serve. they are most submissive, patient, peaceful and virtuous. nor are they quarrelsome, rancorous, querulous, or vengeful." in fact, las casas thought that, in comparison, the spanish looked rather bad. he argued it was the spanish who, in their treatment of the indians, had "surpassed all other barbarians."

the actual debate took place in august of 1550. they met in the old spanish city of valladolid. sepulveda began the debate with a three-hour summary of his long manuscript. las casas had spent years preparing for the debate and had already read sepulveda's manuscript. the day after sepulveda's summary, las casas appeared before the judges with a manuscript of his own. he proceeded to read his manuscript, word for word. his reading lasted five days.

a year later, in may of 1551, sepulveda was given a chance to reply to las casas's arguments. las casas then had a further chance to respond. after intense thought and argument and many attempts to make a final decision, the judges gave up trying to settle the debate. neither side won but soon after the debate began in 1550, the formal suspension of conquest was lifted.

the tendency among scholars today is to say that each side produced a distorted image of indians, and the two views are mirror images of each other, equally false.

i would say, however, that we shouldn't miss the trees for the forest here. of course, what las casas had to say was almost a mirror opposite of sepulveda; after all, they were debating. las casas had to refute sepulveda point by point. more importantly, what was the effect of their opinions? sepulveda's argument justified wholesale slaughter of indians. las casas's argument, had it won the day, might have prevented that slaughter.

i think historians today are wrong to say both sepulveda and las casas were equally wrong. if history involves making judgments about the actions of people, we cannot put las casas and sepulveda in the same boat. sepulveda was an apologist for the king, las casas a defender of indians, neither produced a compelling, 'realistic' description of indigenous people. sepulveda's name is known to a few historians and classicists who speak highly of his contribution to carrying on the western civic humanist tradition. there are no great monuments in his honour that i know of. las casas's name is popularly known and revered, especially in south and central america, where most cities have streets named after him among other monuments and honours. this is as it should be. las casas's *a short history of the conquest of the americas* is as short as its title promises and well worth the read. it was an interesting moment in european intellectual history that, in effect, put to test the moral value of european reason. if you want to read more about the debate, try lewis hanke's *all mankind is one.*

famous kidnappers

although historians have called europeans like columbus *explorers* and *discoverers*, since they didn't actually discover anything perhaps we should think of new names. one that springs to my mind is *kidnappers*.

one of the major, consistent activities of virtually all the 'great' men from europe who first crossed the atlantic was to take native people as prisoners. native prisoners were captured by force and taken back to europe where they were put on display as exotic 'curiosities.'

as well as capturing indians as curiosities, indians were needed as translators. most of the captors hoped their prisoners would survive, learn a european language, and return to the new world to act as interpreters. in the canadian context, it's well known that jacques cartier carried off chief donnacona and between six and ten other haudenosaunee people on his second voyage (1536), after having taken donnacona's sons, domagaya and taignoagny, on his first voyage.

in his search for gold or a northwest passage, martin frobisher, another man often known as an 'explorer' and 'discoverer,' captured several inuit in the 1570s. george best, his shipmate, described how it was done: "for knowing well how they greatly delighted in our toyes, and specially in belles, he rang a pretie lowbel, making wise that he would give him the same that would come and fetch it.... when he thought to take at the captain's hand he was thereby taken himself; for the captain being readily provided, let the bel fal and cought the man fast, plucking him with maine force boate and al into his bark out of the sea."

lying and treachery were all in a day's work for these great european men. frobisher's captive was 'displayed' on the river thames, kayak and all, where he was encouraged to hunt swans for the amusement of watching crowds. He, too, died of european care. stephen greenblat has written an interesting, scholarly, and theoretical book that deals with these issues, called *marvelous possessions.*

history is carried by bodies: konwatsi?tsiaienni and thayendanegea

once europeans began to colonize the americas, it was not long before indians were affected by european politics. konwatsi?tsiaienni (mary or molly brant) and her younger brother, thayendanegea (joseph brant), were prominent mohawk leaders who became paricularly influential during the american revolution. while her brother is better known, konwatsi?tsiaenni was an important leader in her own right. loyalties among the iroquois were split between the europeans and their wars, first the british against the french (the seven years war) and, later, the american colonists (the american revolutionary war). haudenosaunee nations held the balance of power in these struggles; as allies they were valued; as enemies, feared. the cayuga nation was pro-british, while the tuscarora and oneida nations were pro-american. both the seneca and onondaga were divided.

thayendanegea had travelled to england in 1775, where he was wined and dined by british high society. this, and konwatsi?tsiaienni's marriage to william johnson, undoubtedly helps explain why they helped persuade the mohawks to adopt a pro-british policy.

a seneca named sayenqueraghta had the role of leading war chief among the haudenosaunee nations, and another seneca, otatiani sagoyewotha ("he who keeps them awake"), also known as red jacket, was thayendanegea's biggest opponent. he was a great speaker and military leader who went from the british to the american side, though he wanted the seneca nation to be neutral.

one of the things thayendanegea is most known for is his activity after the wars. when the british lost the war, they had to find some way of looking after their allies. they bought a large piece of land from the mississaugas and turned over the biggest part of it, about six miles on each side of the grand river, to thayendanegea and his followers. the land allowed thayendanegea and about 1,800 iroquoian followers to settle down, and formed the basis of the modern six nations reserve in southern ontario, near brantford. this involved the lands that were recently subject to a serious dispute near caledonia, ontario. thayendanegea devoted much time to rebuild the six nations confederacy and to provide economic stability for his people. he died in 1807. a biography of thayendanegea, called *joseph brant 1743-1807: man of two worlds,* has been written by isabel thompson kelsay.

the treaty of treaties

the *royal proclamation of 1763* was the first major british policy statement for territory that would become canada. it has never been revoked. it has the force of a legal statute that has not been overturned. some scholars say it could have constitutional force, and the *royal proclamation of 1763* is reaffirmed by name in the canadian *constitution act, 1982.* so it is very important not only in understanding the history of colonization and indian struggle against it, but for dealing with our current law and land disputes.

in europe in 1763, the seven years' war between england and france ended with the signing of the treaty of paris. in the americas, the french colonies had been defeated by the british in 1759, at the battle of bunglers (the english general wolfe moved too far, too fast, and could have been trapped; the french general montcalm left his protected fortress to fight when he could have waited) on the plains of abraham, at quebec city.

the treaty of paris turned "new france" over to the english. the territory came with some serious problems to deal with, none more serious than establishing good relations with aboriginal peoples. the english defeated the french in america with the aid of their indian allies. just because the french surrendered, their indian allies were not sure they had to do the same. in fact, they also did not think the french really had the right to surrender "new france" at all, since it was indian land. in order to calm both their indian allies and potential enemies, the english decided to make a strong promise to indian peoples that aboriginal rights would be respected.

on october 7, the *royal proclamation of 1763* was announced. it contains a very strong statement in support of what we would today call aboriginal rights. it is still frequently mentioned by first nations in support of their land claims. basically, the proclamation says that "all the lands and territories lying to the westward of the sources of the rivers which fall into the sea [atlantic] from the west and north west" were to be reserved for the use of aboriginal people and could not be taken from them, unless they were willing to surrender the land. if native people were willing to surrender it, only the crown (or government) could buy it, and it had to follow a procedure that involved assembling all the indians, having them choose a leader, and paying a fair price.

the *royal proclamation of 1763* is a legal document written in typical language of the eighteenth century, so in some cases it's very difficult to interpret. it's clear, though, that the most basic implication of the proclamation is the policy of protection.

the british were concerned that their own colonies would try to take the native peoples' land, and that this could anger native peoples so much that there would be a costly war. to prevent this, the proclamation tried to set out a firm policy that recognized and respected aboriginal peoples' land ownership. the british went so far as to say they would throw settlers off indian lands if those settlers were on unceded or unsurrendered land.

interestingly, when the thirteen colonies that became the united states decided to fight the british, one of the issues was that the american colonists did not want to respect indian land ownership and wanted to be able to settle on any land. historians in the usa say it was a revolution over tea and taxes, but it was also a revolution against aboriginal rights.

in the usa, aboriginal rights had to be won through the courts and the famous marshall decisions in the early nineteenth century. in canada, aboriginal rights now recognized by the government begin with the *royal proclamation of 1763*, which still had force in british north america after the american revolution.

the proclamation is only a few pages long. about half of it deals with the new french-speaking colonies in louisiana and new france (quebec) that the british acquired. the other half of it deals with aboriginal peoples. on this basis, it could be said that, in the founding of canada, our country was seen not as a merger between two peoples, but as founded on the principle of living in peace and with respect between three peoples – the english, the french, and the many first nations of this country. anthony hall has written a huge study, *the american empire and the fourth world*, the first volume of which offers a lot of history regarding the proclamation.

interpreting the proclamation: why can't words just mean what they say?

lawyers and scholars argue about three things concerning the royal proclamation today. the first question is whether aboriginal rights were simply recognized by the royal proclamation or if the king *created* aboriginal rights in this document.

in 1763, when king george declared that the crown (or government) would try to protect aboriginal peoples from settlers and colonists, was he creating those rights, which then existed only after the royal proclamation was written? or was he observing that native peoples had rights they had not surrendered, which pre-existed any documents written by any government?

while it might seem abstract, this is an important question. if the royal proclamation is a source of aboriginal rights, then aboriginal rights are created by government and therefore could be taken away by the government. if the proclamation recognized aboriginal rights that were never surrendered, then those rights could only be surrendered or limited by aboriginal peoples themselves, not by anyone else – including government.

to be honest, there is no real answer to this in the proclamation itself. at one point, the document says 'until our further pleasure be known,' which suggests that the king thought he could change his mind about aboriginal rights. but that statement is in a minor clause and it would be stretching it a lot to say it should apply to the whole document.

to me, it doesn't make sense to think of aboriginal rights as given to aboriginal people. instead we should acknowledge that they always had these rights, but this argument takes us beyond the proclamation. interestingly, this issue – pre-existing or existing rights – was one of the most important items debated at the constitutional talks in the 1980s, so it's still topical. and native leaders rightly insist that their rights do not come from the proclamation, but rather from the fact that native peoples lived here for centuries before the arrival of europeans.

a second argument about the royal proclamation is the question of where it should apply. does it apply to all 'aboriginal' peoples and regions even those like the denendeh, since in 1763 the king didn't know denendeh existed? could he write a policy that should apply there? the alberta government says the royal proclamation doesn't apply to the lubicon; the bc government, as i will discuss later, says the proclamation doesn't apply to the nisga'a or most of bc.

this is also a very topical question. in 1763, denendeh and most of northwestern canada were *terra incognita* (unknown lands) to the english, though they may have been legally covered by the hudson's bay company's charter. but the proclamation says "[all] the lands and territories lying to the westward of the sources of the rivers which fall into the sea from the west and north west." literally, "all the lands" include denendeh. also, if the proclamation has constitutional force, then it should apply to the whole country, not just part of it.

you could say that as a british policy, as long as it has not been revoked (and it hasn't), the royal proclamation is meant to apply everywhere the british apply their policy as they establish jurisdiction in that area.

the third debate about the proclamation is: does the document imply that aboriginal people were sovereign or self-governing?

the proclamation talks about aboriginal people as "nations with whom we are connected." this strongly suggests that, in 1763, the king recognized that the crown's relationship with aboriginal peoples was between sovereign nations. but the proclamation, in the very same sentence, refers to native people as "tribes ... who live under our protection," which suggests the british saw them as subjects or wards (children) of the government.

the most reasonable interpretation of this phrase, i would suggest, is that the proclamation dealt with native peoples in both ways. those who lived in indian territory would be seen as nations; those who lived within the boundries of the colonies would be seen as "under the protection" of the crown.

so there are no easy answers within the proclamation to these three important, topical questions. yet the royal proclamation of 1763 contains a strong statement of aboriginal rights and firmly establishes that canada is founded on three groups of cultures: english, french, and aboriginal.

it is particularly strong on the question of aboriginal title to land. as our constitution developed, as i will discuss later, with the *bna act* of 1867 and the *constitution act, 1982*, aboriginal people are discussed in three sections and a few lines, but a close study of our past shows this wasn't always so. that is why native leaders insisted that the constitution specifically mention the *royal proclamation of 1763*.

the fur trade, or, can a few centuries be summed up in a few paragraphs?

gold and an easy path to china: that's what the french and english were looking for in their early years in the americas. a short cut to china would have been good for trade; the spanish had found lots of gold far to the south. these endeavours and european settlement of the northern part of the americas were paid for by trade in furs with aboriginal peoples. beaver felt was the main material used in hat making, and hats were very useful for keeping your head dry in places like rainy england. beaver was once plentiful in europe, but had been hunted to extinction by the middle ages. so by the 1600s, aboriginal people in what is now northern canada became the world's main supplier of beaver pelts.

historians have written much about the struggle between the northwest and hudson's bay companies, the so-called explorers such as radisson or hearne, the different fur trading posts on 'isolated' lakes and rivers. but for the first hundred years of canadian history, historians often conveniently ignored a very simple fact. the labour, the actual work of hunting and trapping beaver, preparing hides and transporting them to posts, was all done by native women and men.

from the early 1600s to the late 1800s, fur was by far canada's leading export. profit made from fur paid for settlers, fur trading posts, and so-called exploration. the fur trade made canada self-sufficient and profitable. the native people who participated in the fur trade were not foolish traders who were easily ripped off, but generally pretty clever at getting what they wanted. they mostly wanted guns and ammunition to make hunting easier, and copper pots and kettles to make cooking easier.

you may have seen movies in which a native person had to pile beaver furs as high as the musket he wanted to buy. that sort of thing probably actually happened, but rarely. there was a standard rate for muskets of a few prime beaver pelts.

until about 1760, most native trappers also had the choice of whether they would trade with the french or the english (and, later, the northwest company or the hudson's bay company). native trappers could always go to the other traders for a better price. since they were the only suppliers of furs, both traders had to be careful they didn't aggravate native people too much.

but, after 1821, the two companies merged into one, and then the hudson's bay company could get away with cheating native people. it began by 'fixing' the weigh scales and mixing flour in with the gunpowder and so on. but this took place in the later part of the fur trade; the companies couldn't get away with it as easily in the early years.

native people also helped europeans by acting as guides and translators, by feeding them when they were hungry, by sometimes curing them when they were sick (especially with scurvy), and by showing europeans how to live in this new country. native people were repaid in the late 1800s by having much of their land taken from them as well as their right to run their own lives.

white people like to think they did all the work to 'improve' canada and produce all its wealth, but we should all remember that for the first 250-odd years of european history in north america, it was the europeans who depended on native people. the hard work of many native women and men provided the economic foundation of this land in its modern form. if you'd like to read more about the fur trade, try the now classic *indians in the fur trade* by arthur ray or *partners in furs* by toby morantz and daniel francis. these books and many others written in the last almost forty years have gone a long way to correcting the earlier silences regarding aboriginal peoples central role in the making of canada.

inuit in canadian history

inuit are a distinct first peoples, formerly called eskimos, who live in the arctic regions of the world, including in what is now the canadian arctic. generally, the history of intensive contact and conflict between inuit and non-natives is comparatively recent. however, inuit ancestors may have been among the first aboriginal americans to encounter europeans because of the norse voyages in the tenth and eleventh centuries.

norse colonizers established a pattern of occupying northern islands along a westward path in the ninth century. from the western scottish islands, they pushed on to iceland, greenland, and eventually north america. the eirikssons probably travelled along the coast of labrador in the early eleventh century, while norse colonists in greenland may have visited ellesmere island in the thirteenth century.

the likely route of norse colonizers to their new-foundland settlement, today called l'anse aux meadows, would have taken them close to baffin island and along the coast of labrador. most of this was arctic terrain, peopled by the dorset, thule, and later inuit cultures.

no one really knows what relations between the norse and the natives they encountered were like. hostility may have been one of the reasons why norse settlement of north america failed. norse legends about skraelings ('savages') emphasized hostility.

on the other hand, there is also evidence of co-operation between the two cultures. since the norse were interested in farming and fishing, while the inuit were hunters, they may not have had much reason to fight. archaeologists have found smelted iron, bronze, and copper in early inuit campsites. this is evidence of trade between the two peoples. the norse had tools to offer, the inuit fur and ivory, so trade could easily have benefitted both sides.

through the fifteenth century, the norse colonies slowly declined and failed, probably because the climate grew colder and trade with europe grew poorer. by the time of columbus, the norse had abandoned their occupation of the american arctic.

so, although intensive contact between inuit and nonnatives did not take place until the late nineteenth and early twentieth centuries, ancestors of the inuit living in the eastern arctic very likely had some exposure to europeans hundreds of years before columbus. while we tend to think of inuit as among the last indigenous americans to encounter europeans, they may well have been the first.

there is a good map of norse voyages and settlement in the *historical atlas of canada. volume one,* edited by harris and matthews.

white fox and seal fur...

the inuit fur trade differed in important ways from the fur trade with other canadian first nations. however, just as in the subarctic, where the fur trade became the most important point of contact and negotiation between native and non-native cultures, in the arctic, the fur trade had a large impact.

the fur trade in southern canada went through several phases, from an early maritime trade on the east coast in the sixteenth century through to its expansion to the pacific and up the mackenzie valley in the nineteenth century. although the fur trade with the inuit took place in the modern fur trade phase, in many respects it more closely resembled the early maritime trade. unlike with aboriginal people in the south, who trapped and traded mostly beaver fur, the inuit fur trade involved first fox fur and eventually seal fur as well.

in the later part of the nineteenth century and in to the twentieth century, most of the trading took place from ships. often, these ships were in arctic waters in order to hunt whales or to fish. while they were in the north, they realized that a tidy profit could be made on the side by trading for furs and other items with the inuit they encountered. soon the ships began stocking supplies specifically for the purpose of trading. they also began making regular stops at points where they knew they could find inuit trappers, or where inuit trappers knew the traders would be. although this sort of sporadic trading could be advantageous to both sides, it often had a harmful impact on the inuit. the case of the mackenzie inuit serves as a useful reminder.

between 1850 and 1900, the lives of the mackenzie inuit, who occupied the coastal region around the mackenzie delta, changed drastically because of the establishment of fort mcpherson. european goods and european diseases began to spread through the area. when american whalers started to visit the area in large numbers, especially after 1890, this process was accelerated. between two measles epidemics in the early 1900s, and the affects of alcoholism and other social problems introduced by the whalers, the mackenzie inuit virtually disappeared as a distinct culture by 1910.

for other inuit cultures, the full intensity of their encounter with european cultures did not come until later and the impacts were not quite as drastic. between 1910 and 1930, traders, including those working with the hudson's bay company, began setting up posts throughout the arctic. the *inuit land use and occupancy project, volume two: supporting studies,* edited by freeman, contains a number of interesting articles on the inuit fur trade, inuit trapping, and the mackenzie inuit.

history is carried by bodies: shawnandithit

shawnandithit was born around the early 1800s. she was a beothuk woman. the beothuk were the first nation who lived in the territory we now know as newfoundland, who were among the first aboriginal people to encounter europeans in what would become canada. the beothuk used a red ochre dye on their skins. some historians believe that indians were called "red men" because the europeans saw beothuk with their skin dyed and then used the expression for all indians.

there were probably never more than 1,000 beothuk. through the eighteenth century, they experienced the worst effects of colonization. diseases, warfare and systematic attacks had almost completely wiped the beothuk out by the time shawnandithit was born. she was raised with her people, who, by then, probably tried to keep away from the europeans as much as possible.

the europeans established permanent fishing villages on the coasts of newfoundland, and were irritated by the beothuk, who would sometimes carry on pilfering raids. apparently, a bounty was placed on beothuk scalps to encourage people to attack the beothuk. by the early nineteenth century, there were very few beothuk left.

shawnandithit was captured by the english with her mother and her sister in the spring of 1823. at the time, the three women were in bad shape. they had barely survived the winter and were starving. the english wanted to return the women to their people with presents and food in order to try to establish more peaceful relations.

but it was too late. no beothuk could be found. when shawnandithit's mother and sister died of tuberculosis, she became the last surviving member of her nation. she was given the christian name nance april and adopted by a farming family headed by john peyton.

in 1828 she was sent to st. john's. there she worked with w.e. cormack, recording information about her people. much of what we know about the beothuk language and culture comes from what shawnandithit told cormack. shawnandithit spent a lot of time in her last years filling her sketchbook with drawings, which still survive. these drawings are well known and provide both knowledge about her people and a testament to her way of seeing. unfortunately, she was not to have much time to do this work.

separated from her people, possibly the last survivor, living with strangers, she died on june 6, 1829. we owe to shawnandithit what little we know about the beothuk. shawnandithit saw her loved ones, her people, her nation, die before her eyes. she witnessed the end to history, the end of all endings, the final futility and failure. last of her people, she would not be the last person in canada to undergo that most painful of all possible human witnessings.

there is a book by j.p. howley called *the beothuks or red indians,* and a good novel, based on history, called *riverrun* by peter such; both of these use shawnandithit's story.

as long as this land shall last

between 1870 and 1921, the government of canada negotiated the numbered treaties, 1 to 11, with the first nations in the north and western part of canada. there are two main reasons the government negotiated these treaties. first, for more than 200 years, native peoples and europeans in this part of the americas had negotiated with each other through the fur trade. there was a long history of peaceful bargaining. this was very different from what went on to the south, where first spaniards and then the united states calvary dealt with indians as obstacles and enemies, waging ruthless warfare against them.

secondly, in 1763 the king of england's royal proclamation promised to respect native peoples' land rights and recognized that native people had title to their land. it could be surrendered or ceded only through negotiations with the government, in which a fair price must be paid.

my old friend, a. rodney bobiwash, a scholar and activist tragically lost to us at an early age, tells us that in 1850, after the great chicago fire, timber was needed from north of the great lakes to rebuild that city. two treaties were signed with anishinabwe peoples to get access to that territory. the main negotiator, william b. robinson, followed the procedures set down in the *royal proclamation of 1763*. the treaties he concluded are known today as the robinson treaties. they became the models for the numbered treaties.

in 1869 the hudson's bay company (hbc) agreed to sell its rights to northwestern canada, then called rupertsland, to canada. the purchase was supposed to take effect december 1, 1869, but louis riel put a stop to that by turning the appointed governor back at the border. this led to the first riel rebellion, which i'll get to later.

the rupertsland purchase was supposed to give canada title to most of the northwest, but native people disagreed. when they heard about the arrangement, they complained, saying the land was not the hbc's to sell. the government decided to deal with their complaints through the treaty process.

as land was needed for settlement, railways, or resource development, the government would meet with aboriginal peoples of that area and negotiate a treaty with them. the eleven numbered treaties signed between 1870 and 1921 covered a huge area of the country. seven of the treaties were negotiated at the rate of about one per year between 1871 and 1877. alexander morris, who was treaty commissioner for treaties 3 to 6, wrote a book about the earlier treaties and his own experience, called *a history of the treaties with the indians of canada*, which is still available in reprint form.

/treaty making was a fairly straightforward process, following the forms that had long been used during the fur trade epoch. a treaty commission would travel to a particular area and let it be known they were there to negotiate a treaty (often these arrangements were made in advance). native people would gather and designate a leader or leaders to speak for them. both sides would make long speeches, mostly about how they wanted to live in peace together. a peace pipe would be smoked. then the terms of the treaty would be discussed. in the early treaties, the process would take days and discussions were long and involved.

even though the treaties were prepared in the east before negotiations, changes could be made. for example, in treaty 6 for saskatchewan, there is a provision, put in at the insistence of the plains cree, that the indian agent keep a medicine chest on hand. in the later treaties, such as treaty 11 in the northwest territories, the process didn't take much more than a day in each of the communities, and the commissioners did not make any changes to the prepared document – though they probably promised to do so.

the written versions of the numbered treaties all look basically the same, though there are some differences. all of them say who the treaty is between: the government of canada and a specific group of first nations. in the written treaties, native people give the government two things: they surrender most of their land and they make a promise of good behaviour. in exchange for this, the first nations were promised reserves, annuities (a set sum of money to be paid every year, sometimes $3, sometimes $5), schools and teachers, hunting and fishing rights on unsurrendered territory, money and supplies to help indians who wanted to try their luck at farming, and an initial payment of money, clothes, supplies, and medals. most of the treaty texts are only three or four pages long. based on reading these written words, the government goes about its business of handing out as little as possible, ignoring hunting rights, administering the poverty it has created and funding research reports to try and understand why things are so bad on so many reserves.

but the treaties are more than these few written pages. they involve what was said during the speeches or negotiations: oral promises which i will discuss below. more even than that, they include a spirit: a spirit of respect, a spirit of peaceful co-existence, a spirit of mutuality, a spirit of fairness, a spirit of justice, a spirit of national integrity, a spirit of honour, a spirit of recognition, a spirit so subtle it quietly lays in wait for the day when it may re-emerge to mend the wounds torn into so much flesh by broken promise after broken promise after broken promise after broken promise. some day, the treaties will be more than lies.

as long as the sun shines

were the treaties a good or a bad deal? it depends on how you interpret them. if you just use the written versions, the treaties seem like pretty bad deals in which native leaders gave up vast chunks of land in exchange for relatively little. but if you listen to the stories of elders and oral traditions of native people, the treaties look a lot better.

if you read any of the treaties today, the promises they make are very limited and vague. hunting and fishing rights, for example, are 'subject to regulations' the government might want to make. treaties also promise education rights, although in the written versions this is limited to maintenance of a school or the salary of a teacher. but, on extinguishment of title to land, the language is strong and clear. in the numbered treaties, aboriginal people promise to "cede, release, surrender and yield up" to the canadian government "all their rights, titles, and privileges whatsoever, forever," to their lands.

because of what the written treaties say, the government claims that when it provides free medical aid, education, or social welfare to native peoples, these are not treaty rights. the government can stop doing so whenever it chooses. for example, when cutbacks were made in the financial support of native students in universities, the government argued this: the only treaty obligation was to provide a school on the reserve and a teacher.

native leaders and elders argue that this narrow view shows no understanding of the spirit of the treaties, which goes beyond what is on paper. most native leaders who signed the treaties (with an x or a clan mark) could not read or write. they agreed to what was verbally promised to them.

in the speeches made at the time of the treaties, native people were promised health care, education, and economic and social assistance as long as they needed it. They were told that the crown was generous and that they could rely on her 'bounty and benevolence' (which is the title of a good book on saskatchewan treaties by arthur ray, james miller and frank tough). these promises were written in the language of the time, but they were meant to apply forever: "as long as the sun shines and the rivers run" was the phrase used by both indian and white people.

treaty indians say the treaties could be a good deal if the government would live up to its side and respect the spirit of the agreements. the treaties would then be seen as a trade: native people gave white people access to huge tracts of land and resources from which the newcomers amassed enormous wealth. and non-native people promised indians health, education, economic development, social assistance, and hunting and fishing rights.

in this conflict between indian and government leaders over the treaties, the two sides can't even agree on what the treaties are. the government says the treaties are contracts made between canada and some of its subjects. native leaders say treaties are signed between nations and that the numbered treaties are international agreements. on this basis, many treaty indians argue that self-government should also be seen as a treaty right.

canada's supreme court will probably end up deciding many of these questions. in a 1990 case involving huron indians who were using wood from a provincial park in quebec (the sioui case), the supreme court agreed that "the treaty must be construed not according to the technical meaning of its words to learned lawyers, but in the sense in which they would naturally be understood by the indians." this really suggests that the courts are leaning toward the spirit of the treaties, even as the government continues its very narrow approach.

of course, in some cases – treaties 8 and 11 in the northwest territories are good examples – native leaders and elders say they did not intend to trade away their title to the land.

as long as the rivers run

in the northwest territories (nwt), dene leaders and elders say they did not extinguish or give up their title to the land when treaties 8 and 11 were negotiated in 1899 and 1921. this view was supported by the northern priest and poet (canada's own liberation theologist), rene fumoleau, in his book *as long as this land shall last*. yet, treaty 8 says, "the said indians do hereby cede, release, surrender and yield up to the government of the dominion of canada, for her majesty the queen and her successors for ever, all their rights, titles and privileges whatsoever, to the lands included within the following limits...." treaty 11 says exactly the same thing, except the land is ceded to the king.

this is a striking example of the difference between what the treaties say in writing and what native people remember about the treaties. this may be in part because the written element of the treaties were not the result of the negotiations. they were usually brought with the treaty commissioners, having been prepared well before the negotiations began.

for the early treaties, changes could come out of the negotiations between the commissioners and the indians, so changes would be made to the written documents. the treaty 3 negotiations were particularly interesting in this regard; there, first nations' leaders raised the annuities from $3 to $5 per year, and raised the land offered from 160 to 640 acres per family.

But, in the nwt, the native people did not pose much military threat to the government, so the commissioners were given less leeway over what they could agree to. the commissioners' job was to get the indians to sign the treaties, and that's what they did. when the commissioners visited dene communities, they probably made many promises to dene leaders, who were worried about losing their hunting and fishing rights. those promises did not make it into the written, signed treaties. as a result, the dene and the government now disagree about what the treaties promised.

the most important part of this argument is over title to land. in 1959 the government sent out a commission "to investigate the unfulfilled promises of treaties 8 and 11." the government was worried because according to the treaties, the dene should have been given reserves – but they were never set up. the nelson commission found that "at a number of meetings indians who claimed to have been present at the time when the treaties were signed stated that they definitely did not recall hearing about the land entitlement in the treaties."

this issue reached the courts in the early 1970s, when the dene tried to block the proposed mackenzie valley pipeline. during the paulette case in 1973, many elders who witnessed the signing of the treaties testified that they heard no mention of land during negotiations. they thought the treaty was a peace and friendship agreement. johnny (jean-marie) beaulieu remembered the commissioners' saying to the people of fort resolution: "we will pay out the treaty to you here and it has no binding on your land or country at all. it has nothing to do with this land."

dene people have consistent, strong memories directly opposed to what the treaty says in writing. although the government disagreed, it was willing to negotiate a new land claim in which extinguishment of dene title was an important clause.

in southern canada, most first nations seem content to recognize that land was surrendered. there the issue is whether the spirit of treaty promises will be fulfilled. there are important exceptions; for example, with treaty 9, elders have said they never surrendered land. descendents of those who signed adhesions to treaty 5 have said they never surrendered land.

for the dene, the surrender clause (one of the main parts of the treaty, at least as the government sees it), is in question. of course, most dene would also argue that the government should live up to the spirit of the promises made in 1899 and 1921. aboriginal scholars have started to question whether it was even possible conceptually, within indigenous worldview, to surrender land; something they very likely didn't even see themselves or anyone else as 'owning.' in order to be polite, i'll only say a few words about water: the surrender clauses in all the numbered treaties only mention land, though in modern treaties those clauses mention lands and waters. hence an argument can be made for the fact that throughout the treaty area first nations still have aboriginal title to all the lakes and rivers they traditionally used and occupied.

the violence of the letter: the st. catherine's milling and lumber company and native land title

a court case in 1883 over whether the st. catherine's milling and lumber company had the right to cut timber in northern ontario became a landmark in aborginal law, regardless of how little the ojibwa peoples in the area had to do with that case. the owners of the company had contributed to john a. macdonald's election campaigns and because this made them 'friends,' the federal government gave them the licence to log. the provincial government said only it had the right to grant licences to cut timber and got a court injunction stopping the company from logging. the land involved in this case was treaty 3 territory. treaty 3 had been negotiated in 1873 between the crown and the ojibwa of northwestern ontario.

the reason why the case became so important to aboriginal people has to do with the federal government's argument. the federal government argued that the *royal proclamation of 1763* had given the ojibwa peoples, and other aboriginal peoples, absolute title to their territories.

because of that, when a treaty was negotiated, the federal government believed it was effectively buying the land from native peoples. if the federal government bought the land, it owned the land and could therefore grant licences to anyone. the provincial government argued instead that only it had the right to grant timber licences because the constitution of canada (the *british north america act* of 1867) gave it that right. it argued that indians had never had outright ownership of the land, but only a kind of partial ownership, which the federal government then bought out through the treaty.

so, in essence, this case involved that famous canadian question: is this a federal or provincial responsibility? this is a question canadian governments have argued about for as long as canada has existed, and they are still arguing, but in the 1880s, the way the question was debated involved the crucial question of aboriginal title. the st. catherine's milling case hinged on how the courts would interpret the royal proclamation, the treaties, and the *bna act.*

remember that by 1883, when the case began, seven of the eleven numbered treaties had been negotiated. this case would determine what those treaties meant, and how the government would view so-called 'unsurrendered land' in the future. perhaps as noteworthy as the final decision in the case, it is crucial to point out that native people had no direct say. there were lawyers for the federal government, lawyers for the province, and lawyers for the company busily arguing about aboriginal title. but no chiefs, no elders, not even lawyers, were present to speak for the treaty 3 indians. perhaps, in this case, justice was not only blind, but deaf!

in 1888 the judicial committee of the privy council in england, then acting as the highest court of the commonwealth and therefore canada, handed down its decision. the committee ruled against the federal government. the court said that the *royal proclamation of 1763* did not confer complete and total title to aboriginal peoples, but, instead, a more limited title that acts as a 'burden' upon the crown. this is what the court said: "the tenure of the indians was a personal and usufructuary right, dependent upon the good will of the sovereign. the lands reserved are expressly stated to be 'parts of our dominions and territories'; and it is declared to be the will and pleasure of the sovereign that, 'for the present,' they shall be reserved for the use of the indians as their hunting grounds, under his protection and dominion."

the court, quoting the royal proclamation, decided that aboriginal people did not have outright ownership of their traditional lands. instead, the crown had an underlying ownership and aboriginal title was a kind of surface title that involved usufructuary rights (a "usufructuary" right involves a right to use but not own something). the court was saying that natives had a right to hunt and fish on the land without owning it.

st. catherine's milling is, therefore, a case that severely limited the legal way of understanding aboriginal title. the courts did not expand in any detail on what aboriginal title or rights meant. in fact, they said (and this is my personal favourite saying of canadian legal history): "there was a great deal of learned discussion at the bar with respect to the precise quality of the indian right, but their lordships do not consider it necessary to express any opinion upon the point."

native people, without being there or being represented, lost this crucial case. we don't have to agree with the privy council or its interpretation of treaties and the proclamation, but it set an important precedent that courts and governments have still refused to break. of course, if we were to think of justice with a sense of basic moral principles, there was a great deal wrong with the decision. people from one culture were using their own rules to tell people from another what rights they had. and even then, they were applying their own rules unfairly. james youngblood (sakej) henderson, an indigenous legal scholar who has expressed admiration for the basic principles of british justice, has written, "in its approach to the rights of native people the law becomes tyranny at worst and an ineffective apologist at best. the canadian governments may call it law, but it is racism." the decision in st. catherine's milling fits this description.

there are many books that deal with aboriginal title and most of them refer to st. catherine's milling. two good ones are *aboriginal peoples and the law,* edited by bradford

morse, and *the quest for justice*, where you can find henderson's article, edited by menno boldt and j. anthony long.

those members of the judicial committee of the privy
council were no doubt respected, churchgoing men (all
men!). no doubt they were praised and honoured and
enjoyed lives of privilege. yet, with a few strokes of the
pen, they set the terms that, to this day, justify continuing racist conquest in canada. never in their lives were
they faced with the consequences of their actions. though
they will not face it, there is one consequence they cannot
avoid: we, who bear their questionable legacy, will burn
the letters of their names in the annals of infamy. our history will know them only as leeches whose smug judgments were as far from justice as they themselves were
from being humane.

there were indian acts even before there was canada

the *indian act* of 1876 was actually nothing very new. it
restated and consolidated earlier laws respecting indian
peoples. before 1867, the government's policy toward
indians hinged on two main ideas: protection and civilization. the idea of protection stemmed from the *royal
proclamation of 1763*. the government tried in these early

years to protect indian lands from being trespassed on or stolen. for example, in 1839 a law was passed in upper canada (now ontario) to protect indian lands from trespassers and from seizure for non-payment of debt. this law was amended a year later, when indian land was designated as crown land, held in trust for native people and therefore free of taxation.

then, the idea of protection seemed good: the government sided with native people against unscrupulous non-natives. of course, the government was also taking lands away from indians through the treaty process. but the lands that indians got, such as reserves, were to be carefully protected. in part, these laws formed the basis of the government's trust relationship with native peoples – it was supposed to act on their behalf.

slowly, this policy of protection evolved into a damaging paternalism. the government felt it knew what was best for indians. for example, in 1850 a law was passed in upper canada, banning the sale of alcohol to indians. in lower canada (now quebec) in the same year, for the first time, a law was passed defining who indians were. although this law was very broad (it included "all persons of indian ancestry, all persons married to such persons, belonging to or recognized as belonging to an indian band, and living with the band"), it meant the government felt it had the power to say who was, and who was not, an indian.

the other basic idea behind indian policy was that indians needed to be civilized, under a non-native definition of civilization. in the early 1800s, under the influence of the anti-slavery movement in britain and early evangelical christian revivals in the usa, teaching indians so-called civilization meant just teaching enough so they would not frighten their non-native neighbours.

later, 'civilization' came to mean more than teaching aboriginal people to dress like white people, but also to live like them. that is, it came to mean assimilation. in 1857, "an act to encourage the gradual civilization of the indians of this province" was passed by the united canadas. the first part of this 'civilization act' said its purpose was to civilize and integrate indians. the act defined who indians were, still in a very broad way, and then took away their rights as citizens unless they could read or write english or french, be free of debt, and be of "good moral character." of course, many, perhaps most, non-natives in the canadas could not meet the criteria mentioned above.

this 'civilization act' in many ways was the first full-fledged indian act. it established what historian john tobias called the basic paradox of all future indian policy: separation in order to assimilate. tobias wrote, "the legislation to remove all legal distinctions between indians and euro-canadians actually established them [these distinction]." two good collections of essays are available with articles on many of the topics i've covered. one is called *as long as the sun shines and water flows*, edited by ian a.l. getty and antoine s. lussier. it has a good general article on the treaties by george stanley, a copy of the *royal proclamation of 1763*, and articles by john tobias and john milloy on early indian acts. another good collection is called *out of the background*, edited by robin fisher and kenneth coates. it has good articles on the fur trade by arthur ray and bruce trigger, and on women in the fur trade by sylvia van kirk.

history is carried by bodies: mistahimaskwa

mistahimaskwa (big bear) was one of canada's great aboriginal leaders who was not understood or appreciated by non-natives during his lifetime. he was born around 1825 of cree and ojibwa parents. it was the cree of the plains whom he came to lead. hugh dempsey has written a biography of him, called *big bear: the end of freedom.*

mistahimaskwa had a very strong bearing, by all accounts. he had a great voice and was known to be a skilled hunter as a young man. he was particularly good at being able to shoot from under the neck of his horse while riding at full speed. this was a useful skill for hunting buffalo and for plains warfare. mistahimaskwa was known for distrusting the whites, who feared him, and for struggling for unity among indian peoples. although his hostility towards non-natives made him a radical, he generally sought peace and tried to find ways of preventing violence. however, in the canadian plains of the late nineteenth century, violence was almost unavoidable.

in 1870 mistahimaskwa was part of a major cree and assiniboine war party against their ancient foes in the blackfoot confederacy. their attack on the blood camp near fort whoop-up failed when the blood were reinforced by the piegan. both the blood and piegan had much more modern repeating rifles. they inflicted terrible losses on the cree, who, a year later, were forced into negotiating peace with these old enemies.

mistahimaskwa attended the negotiations for treaty 6 in 1876. he refused to accept presents at the beginning, saying he did not want to put a rope around his neck. many people said later this had to do with his fear of hanging, but others now think he was worried about his people's becoming trapped. the terms of treaty 6 were not agreeable to mistahimaskwa. he did not like the fact that canadian laws would rule over the plains cree, which would take away from the people's ability to govern themselves. so he refused to sign the treaty or take treaty money.

in the next few years, mistahimaskwa hunted further to the south, in the last remaining areas where buffalo could be found. he met with louis riel in 1880. riel helped him get the agreement of american indians to let him hunt on their reserves. after 1882 the american army refused to allow the canadian indians to hunt in the usa so, with the buffalo quickly disappearing and few alternatives in sight, and with his people growing hungry, he was effectively forced to sign the treaty in 1882.

in 1884 mistahimaskwa organized a thirst dance (sun dance) at poundmaker's reserve. over 2,000 of the people came. as well as wanting the occasion to be a spiritual renewal, mistahimaskwa wanted the people to come together on one big reserve in saskatchewan. the government was suspicious of this and wouldn't allow it. soon after, they amended the *indian act*, restricting the movements of indians and banning outright ceremonies like the sundance.

at the time of the metis rebellion of 1885, as mistahimaskwa was losing control of his band, a group of his followers was responsible for the killings at frog lake on april 2, which i will discuss later. mistahimaskwa himself tried to prevent the killings and his efforts saved some lives, but this was overlooked by the government during his later trial.

after batoche, mistahimaskwa and his remaining followers avoided the canadian military by going into the bush. there was a short battle on may 27 when the nwmp interrupted a thirst dance of his band. on july 2 mistahimaskwa surrendered to a very surprised guard by walking into fort carlton. one of the greatest indignities that happened to mistahimaskwa was the fact that his hair was cut short when he was imprisoned for his supposed part in the uprising, along with poundmaker and one arrow. mistahimaskwa was released after half of his three-year sentence, because his health was giving out. he died within a few months of his release in 1888.

'indians and lands reserved for indians'

in 1867 canada became a new nation. a law was passed, the *british north america act* (*bna act*), which gave the new government of canada the power to govern itself. british north america was what europeans called the parts of the continent that britain still controlled after the american revolution of 1776.

the english wouldn't have dreamed of using indian names for what they called british north america. however, the name "canada" probably derives from a haudenosaunee word, though no one knows for certain. the story goes that when cartier travelled down the st. lawrence river in the 1530s, he came upon a village. when he asked what this place was called, the people thought he meant the community, and responded with the word "kanata," iroquoian for "village."

the *bna act* became the key document in canada's constitution, and, unlike the *royal proclamation of 1763*, about half of which deals with indian issues, the *bna act* has very little to say about canada's first nations. only one line of it is about indians. but, that line is very important. section 91 lists the responsibilities of the federal government, while line 24 on the list says: "indians and lands reserved for indians." so, section 91 (24) of the *bna act* constitutionally ensures that indians are a federal, not a provincial, responsibility.

that the 'highest' level of government, the federal government, would have responsibility over indian affairs was in line with the king's earlier notion contained in the royal proclaimation that taking more land from indians would always be a central feature of 'settlement' and this included the notion that the federal government could also best serve indian interests.

section 91 (24) is the constitutional basis of what is called the trust (or fiduciary) relationship between indians and the federal government. of course, we know that in the 140-odd years since the *bna act,* the federal government has rarely lived up to its constitutional commitment. what most people aren't aware of is that ottawa has consistently tried to unload its responsibility for indians onto provincial governments. the white paper policy of 1969 and the nielsen report of 1985 both recommended turning services for indians over to the provinces. this is something indian leaders have fought long and hard against.

in 1939 the supreme court of canada decided that the word "indian" in the *bna act* applied to inuit (then called eskimo) people as well. at that time, it was not applied to the metis. there are two recent books that focus on federal responsibility for indians and on section 91 (24) of the *bna act.* they are both collections of scholarly essays. one is called *governments in conflict?* edited by j. anthony long and menno boldt. the other is *aboriginal peoples and government responsibility,* edited by david hawkes. the kanata story comes from olive dickason's *the myth of the savage.*

(dis)enfranchising indians: a dangerously subversive story

canada's first major piece of legislation dealing with indians was an "act for the gradual enfranchisement of indians" in 1869. called the *enfranchisement act,* it was canada's first indian act, though the first with that name was not passed until 1876. a dictionary's definition of enfranchisement is "to give (a person) the right to vote in elections." the franchise is the vote, but it can also be understood to mean full citizenship rights. there is an excellent chapter on early indian legislation in robin brownlie's very good book on the history of indian agents called *a fatherly eye.*

the *enfranchisement act* set in place two important processes that would affect indian people pretty much to the present. one was the idea of enfranchisement itself; the other was sexual discrimination. the *enfranchisement act* worked the same way as the *civilization act* of 1857: it defined indians as having less rights than other citizens and invented a way for them to regain their citizen-rights.

there were two kinds of enfranchisement – voluntary and involuntary. voluntary meant it was applied for, in most cases because people wanted to vote or have other rights. involuntary enfranchisement was a new invention of the 1869 act. it meant the government gave citizen-rights to certain indians, whether they wanted them or not. most indians probably did not want to be enfranchised. even though they would gain rights as canadian citizens, they did not want to lose their identity as indians. but the government wanted all indians enfranchised. it was a way to assimilate them. not enough indians applied to be enfranchised after 1857, so the government started to do it automatically after 1869.

the second important creation of the *enfranchisement act* was sexual discrimination. in most first nations' communities, women were highly respected and had full political rights. haudenosaunee women, in fact, had great political authority. but the people who ran the government of canada had different ideas. in the last half of the nineteenth century, canada was influenced by the same victorian ideas that dominated england. in that framework, women were supposed to be "angels of the household," seen but not heard, treated with very little respect. the government thought indian women should have the same role.

so, in 1869, sex discrimination was added to indian legislation. indian women who married non-native men were involuntarily enfranchised. they lost their status as indians. since no women in canada were allowed to vote, they did not gain much, did they? and an indian man who married a non-native woman did not lose his status; in fact, his non-aboriginal wife gained status. i recommend a short book by kathleen jamieson called *indian women and the law in canada: citizen's minus.* as a result of the 1869 *enfranchisement act,* many indian people were forcibly kicked off their reserves. for many years afterward, the department of indian affairs listed at the end of its annual reports the number of indians enfranchised that year. the department saw enfranchisement as the statistical measure of its success.

when the 1869 act did not work to the government's satisfaction, it amended the law to increase the number of people who could be involuntarily enfranchised. both enfranchisement and sex discrimination stayed on the books until 1985, when *bill c-31* changed things, but we'll get back to this later.

the real story here is not of 'enfranchisement,' but of 'status.' the government did not define indians as indians in order to give them indian 'status.' it defined them as indians as a legal tool, in order to take measures against them. instead of wanting to be enfranchised, instead of lining up to apply to gain canadian citizenship, in one of the great unwritten episodes of canadian history, the vast majority of indians voted with their feet on whether they wanted rights as canadian citizens or rights as indians: they were massively in favour of remaining indian. that was how indian 'status' was invented, not by the laws of the powerful, but by the actions and choices of many indigenous people. the people turned a law designed for the purpose of eradicating indians into a law that could do the opposite – legally maintaining a distinct identity. it's quite the trick, subverting the law. if only we can figure out how it works!

when is an inuk an indian, and when is she not an indian?

on july 31, 1880, the british government approved an order-in-council that transferred "all british territories and possessions in north america, not already included in the dominion of canada, and all islands adjacent to any such territories or possessions." the order-in-council specifically excluded newfoundland. this meant that britain, probably the world's foremost 'great power' at the time, transferred and recognized canada's control of the arctic islands to its north. to the extent that those islands were occupied, they were occupied by inuktitut-speaking inuit. neither canada nor britain saw fit to consult with the inuit over this transfer.

although it was happy to assume control over the arctic islands, canada was not really interested in developing a responsible policy towards the people who lived there. in fact, its biggest concern in the first few decades of its control was to make sure no other country tried to take some of the land away from it. while the *bna act* of 1867 had given the federal government responsibility for "indians and lands reserved for Indians," it said nothing about the inuit. this was not a problem as long as the inuit were self-sufficient. but the more they were drawn into the fur trade, the more they began to rely on outsiders for support to tide them over in bad years. and so, the question of who was responsible became a problem.

in the first few decades of the twentieth century, inuit affairs was a kind of football, kicked around from department to department with very little thought. in the early 1920s, inuit were made a responsibility of the indian affairs branch, but within six years, responsibility for inuit was turned back over to the newly reformed northwest territories council. the problem of who had responsibility for inuit reached a climax in the early 1930s. at that time the government of quebec refused to continue paying the cost of relief for inuit who lived in northern quebec, saying that they should be classed as indians and were in the federal government's jurisdiction.

the federal government disagreed. so they went to court. in the mid-1930s, the supreme court was asked to decide if inuit were 'indians' as that term was used in the *bna act*. the case was called *re: eskimos* ("eskimos" was the word used at the time to describe the people we now know as inuit).

the supreme court of canada decided the case in 1939. it relied on all sorts of reports, maps, and hudson's bay company documents that showed inuit people being considered as another indian tribe. the court said that inuit were a federal responsibility. the government of canada, once it accepted the court's verdict, decided not to apply the *indian act* to inuit, since, by the 1940s, they were unhappy with the way the *indian act* worked. in one law, the *bna act*, where it says 'indian,' it means indian and inuit. in another law, the *indian act*, where it says 'indian,' it means indian and not inuit.

so, while the government wanted to control the artic islands, it was not willing to assume responsibility for dealing with the inuit. it did not negotiate treaties with the inuit, and had to be dragged to court to accept its duty regarding quebec inuit. it would take some serious problems, including starvation, to draw serious government attention and concern for inuit peoples.

meanwhile, on a nearby planet named british columbia

in the early 1990s, the supreme court of british columbia ruled against the gitksan-wet'suwet'en peoples' legal claim that they still had aboriginal title to their traditional lands. that decision was eventually overturned by the supreme court of canada; to understand the issues involved, we have to look at the particular history of aboriginal land ownership in bc.

most first nations in bc did not sign treaties with the crown. only two parts of bc are under treaties. treaty 8, which also covers northern alberta and part of the nwt, stretches over the northeastern corner of bc and on vancouver island there are a few aboriginal communities that signed the so-called "douglas treaties." europeans did not reach bc until the late 1700s (after the *royal proclamation of 1763*). the hudson's bay company got involved in the fur trade there after 1821. in the late 1840s, the hbc's chief factor of fort victoria, on vancouver island, was james douglas. the hbc was given responsibility for colonising and "settling" bc. in 1851 douglas became governor as well as chief factor. he initially applied the same policy that had been adopted in the british colonies on the eastern part of the continent. that policy, embodied in the *royal proclamation of 1763*, included respect for aboriginal title.

following that policy, governor douglas, in the first few years of his office, negotiated treaties with indians living in the northeastern and southeastern parts of vancouver island. however, as the colony expanded to the mainland and the cost of negotiating treaties grew, governor douglas wrote to the colonial office in london, asking for the british to bear the cost of treaties. the british wrote back to douglas in 1858, saying, "i have to enjoin you to consider the best and most humane means of dealing with the native indians."

the british agreed with the policy of recognizing aboriginal title and negotiating treaties, but refused to pay for it! governor douglas would not raise taxes to pay for treaties. he took the alternative of simply refusing to negotiate treaties. as a result, bc indians, except for those who signed treaty 8 in 1899 and those who signed the douglas treaties, did not surrender their aboriginal title to the land. to justify their refusal to negotiate treaties, future governments in bc refused to recognize aboriginal title. they argued that the royal proclamation, which was supposed to recognize aboriginal title over "any lands to the west of the headwaters or sources of rivers flowing into the atlantic ocean," did not have jurisdiction over bc.

in 1861 governor douglas began the process of creating reserves for indians on their traditional settlements. like other reserves, these were designated as lands held in trust for indian people by the crown. so, in bc, reserves were not created as part of the treaty process, as they were in the other western provinces. in 1871 bc became part of canada, and the federal government assumed authority for "indians and lands reserved for indians" in accordance with the *british north america act* of 1867. however, in the deal between bc and canada, the province kept ownership and control of all crown lands. even if the government of canada had been prepared to fight for bc indians' aboriginal title and wanted to sign a treaty with them like the ones it was negotiating across the prairies and the north, it could not get the land from the provincial government.

and, as you might have already guessed, the federal government was not interested in putting up much of a fight for bc indians. this means most bc first nations did not surrender their aboriginal title to their traditional lands. most of the bc indians wanted to negotiate, but the governments refused to listen.

in the early 1990s, the gitksan-wet'suwet'en tried to correct this injustice and have their aboriginal title recognized by going to bc's supreme court. chief justice mceachern upheld the colonialist attitudes of nineteenth-century settlers, arguing that early bc laws "exhibit a clear and plain intention to extinguish aboriginal interests." but the only "clear and plain intention" to "extinguish" aboriginal interests would be a treaty. no such treaty was ever signed with the gitksan-wet'suwet'en. mceachern's decision is a throwback to nineteenth-century colonial and racist attitudes and ideas. it is out of step with legal decisions and current understandings of justice of the 1990s, but the gitksan-wet'suwet'en had to spend millions of dollars to take the case to the supreme court of canada to get justice, and set the basis for the nisga'a settlement. a very good book on aboriginal rights in bc, published in the 1990s, is *aboriginal peoples and politics* by paul tennant.

the shifting sands upon which lasting legislation was built

the first *indian act* to go by that name in canada was passed in 1876. it was not very different from the 1869 *enfranchisement act* (or the 1857 *civilization act*). the 1876 *indian act* brought together, or consolidated, previous laws about indian people in one blanket piece of legislation. one new thing the 1876 *indian act* introduced was the idea of a "location ticket." it was a parcel of land an indian man could live on and farm. if he farmed the land for three years, he could then become enfranchised: lose his status as an indian and gain full rights as a canadian citizen. there are two points i want to make about the 1876 *indian act*. first, as a blanket piece of legislation, the *indian act* governed many aspects of indian peoples' lives. it said who was or was not an indian. it imposed rules about everything from inheritance to where people could live. and the *indian act* was never mentioned during any of the treaty negotiations. in understanding the treaties, we should always keep in mind that the chiefs who signed them were never told: "after you sign this your lives will be controlled by a law written in ottawa, a law that only politicians will have the power to change."

the second point i want to make has to do with the ideas behind the *indian act*. one of the main ones was that indians were a "vanishing race." that is the name of a famous photograph taken by american photographer, e.s. curtis, which shows a group of navajo horsemen riding off into the sunset. it was meant to convey the idea that indians were disappearing, and would soon be gone from the americas. it is easy to see how people could have had that idea in the late nineteenth century. the numbers of indians in both the usa and canada were decreasing dramatically, due mostly to warfare and disease, but also to enfranchisement, whereby they no longer 'counted' as indians.

so the *indian act* was based on the belief that within one or two generations, thirty or forty years, there would be no more indians. it was not a law designed to last over 100 years. it was a law meant to last thirty years or less. the *indian act* – and this is still with us today although in a revised form – was built on a foundation of sand. it was built on the notion that indians were a vanishing race, a notion that has obviously proven to be false, let alone offensive and unjust.

despite this, up to the late 1960s, government officials tried to fight the so called "indian problem" by "solving" it through assimilation within a generation or two. they made up a problem and every few years spent millions on new reports to dream up another instant solution, which didn't work and led them to spend millions more. sound familiar?

meaner than scrooge: how the government of canada banned christmas

in many respects, the fifty-odd years after the passing of the *indian act* in 1876 were among the worst that aboriginal people in canada were to experience. the decline of the fur trade, the disappearance of the buffalo, the so-called opening up of the canadian northwest to massive immigration from europe, the negotiation of the numbered treaties and the failure of the riel rebellions all took place in the period between 1870 and 1930.

we should not lose sight of the fact that an important historical shift also took place in this period. before 1870, indian relations with whites were mostly economic in nature. the fur trade was the main point of contact between natives and non-natives. this meant that whites needed native people, who were the main suppliers of fur. so the relations between native and non-natives were interdependent; each side needed the other.

after the decline of the fur trade, those relations shifted. indian relations with whites became primarily political in nature. after 1870 it was the government, not the hudson's bay company, that dominated indian affairs in canada. since indians were less important economically, interdependence was weakened. of all the blows that indians felt in this period, the greatest and longest lasting may have been the imposition by government of the *indian act*. while the actual 1876 *indian act* introduced little in the way of new measures, amendments that followed it were ruthless in their determination to attack aboriginal culture and identity.

in the 1880s, a 'pass system' was established making it illegal for indians to leave their reserves without the indian agent's written permission. in 1884 both the sundance and the potlach, ceremonies crucial to the cultures of plains and pacific coast first nations, respectively, were banned by law. anyone practising these ceremonies could be fined or jailed. because this amendment just listed the ceremonies by name, in 1895 the amendment was revised to ban them by description.

the description states that "every indian...who engages in, or assists in celebrating...any indian festival, dance or other ceremony of which the giving away or paying or giving back of money, goods or articles of any sort forms a part or is a feature...is guilty of an indictable offense and is liable to imprisonment...." talk about mean-spirited, this could have meant that christmas and birthday presents were made illegal for indians! although the government did not prosecute many indians for practising the sundance or potlach, its prosecution of some created the real threat to all indians and native culture. similarly, the pass system was not systematically enforced but depended a great deal on local circumstances; it was mostly applied on the prairies and even there likely only until the thirties. however, these amendments stayed on the books until 1951 and remained as possible social, political and cultural control weapons in the government's arsenal until that time.

imposing a democracy that doesn't deserve the name

one of the most remarkable features of early indian legislation was the development and imposition of the electoral band system. this involved a complicated process. many amendments to the *indian act* were made and a separate law, the *indian advancement act*, was also passed in 1884.

the first move in this story took place in an amendment to the *indian act* in 1880. sections 72 to 74 of the revised *indian act* provided for electoral band governments. section 72 began: "whenever the governor in council deems it advisable for the good government of a band to introduce the election system of chiefs, he may by order in council provide that the chiefs of any band of indians be elected...." it was not up to the indians to decide whether they wanted this system. it was up to the governor in council to decide for them. even today, the wording of section 74 (1) begins: "whenever he deems it advisable for the good government of a band, the minister may declare by order that after a day to be named therein the council of the band, consisting of a chief and councillors, shall be selected by elections...." so you see, over a hundred years later, some things have not changed very much. in 1880 the government felt it had the right and the power to say what sort of system indians should have. today, in spite of all the talk about self-government, legally, for most status indians, the situation remains almost identical.

elections were imposed on indians. however, not just elections, but the specific formula of an electoral process was decided upon by the government. many traditional leaders were undermined and many traditional political values and ideas were undercut. that was the intention of the band council electoral system. the electoral band council system was not imposed everywhere at the same time, but the government was determined that it would eventually get all indians to follow this system.

at akwesasne, for example, a number of petitions were sent to the government, asking that their traditional political system be respected and challenging the government's authority over them. mohawks were particularly concerned because section 73 of the 1880 *indian act* said that "those entitled to vote at the council or meeting thereof shall be male members of the band...." the mohawk traditions gave women a strong role in chosing leaders. the male voting rules generally attacked the traditional roles of native women everywhere, but were particularly offensive to haudenosaunee peoples. in spite of the strong opposition to the government's system, the government insisted on applying it. in 1899 indian affairs, with the co-operation of the rcmp, forced the electoral system on indians at akwesasne. just by reading over the *indian act* and looking at the changes it went through, you can learn a lot about the early struggle of indians over self-government. there still is not much published information on this aspect of indian history. grand chief michael mitchell has an article in *drumbeat* (edited by boyce richardson) on the imposition of the electoral system at akwesasne.

control those noxious weeds!

the *indian act* of 1876 provided for the election of chiefs "for a period of three years, unless deposed by the governor for dishonesty, intemperance, immorality, or incompetency." the act allowed for traditional "life chiefs" who could be deposed for the same reasons. these reasons were obviously so broad that indian affairs bureaucrats could find an excuse to get rid of any chief they did not like.

in 1880 the government decided it needed to go further in weakening the influence of traditional chiefs. the *indian act* was amended so that where the electoral system had been adopted or imposed, "life chiefs shall not exercise the powers of chiefs unless elected." four years later, in 1884, a new section was added to the act. it said the governor could "set aside" an election where it could be proven that "fraud or gross irregularity was practised." after 1894, deposed chiefs were "declared ineligible for re-election for three years" through another amendment.

all this shows that, although the government said it was developing the electoral system to teach indians about democracy, the real reason for the system was to assimilate indians by undermining the power and authority of traditional leaders. if indians voted in a traditional leader, he or she could be removed by the indian agent on the basis of such vague terms as "immorality or incompetency." when the band did not agree with that assessment, and re-elected the same traditional leaders, the law was changed so that those leaders could not stand for re-election. what type of democracy is that? clearly the government was manipulating the electoral band system to try to get the leaders it wanted. just as clearly, first nations were resisting this.

another important aspect of the electoral band system were the powers held by the chiefs and councils. such powers were "subject to confirmation by the governor in council." in 1876 these were limited to a list of six subjects, including such general areas as "the care of public health, the repression of intemperance and profligacy," and such specific, municipal-type areas as "the prevention of trespass by cattle," and "the establishment of pounds and the appointment of pound keepers." this list was expanded to ten areas in 1879. among the new areas in which bands could "frame rules and regulations" was "the repression of noxious weeds." the bands were also given the power to impose limited punishments on those who violated the band's rules (and allowed noxious weeds to grow!). the power to impose punishments was taken away from the band in 1906 and transferred to the governor in council by another amendment. one other power, meanwhile, had been added to the list in 1880, which was to choose the religious denomination of the schoolteachers.

the reason for all these changes in the electoral system and the limited nature of powers delegated to band councils was summed up by indian affairs' annual report of 1897. it said the department was trying to "do away with the hereditary and introduce an elective system, so making... these chiefs and councillors occupy the position in a band which a municipal council does in a white community."

the system has gone through some changes since then, but the basic structure is, in many ways, remarkably similar. wayne daugherty and dennis madill have written a detailed historical report on these issues called *indian government under indian legislation 1868-1951* as part of the outstanding series of studies published by the diand research branch.

a few words about a big nation: the metis nation

the word 'metis' is french and basically means 'mixed' or 'mixed blood.' properly speaking, in the 1800s, if you used the word 'metis,' you meant someone of french and indian descent; if you used the word 'halfbreed,' you meant someone of english or scottish and indian descent. since many people found the word 'halfbreed' to be insulting, today the word 'metis' tends to be used for both groups.

the metis emerged as a distinct social group, or a new people, in the late eighteenth century. although often the metis are viewed as simply a combination of indian and european cultures, most metis argue that they quickly developed a distinctive and unique culture of their own. the historical record supports this claim and that is why we can speak of the metis as a new people.

the metis quickly developed from kinship bonds in both
european and indian communities into their own society
and culture. although the first metis came from infor-
mal marriages normally between non-native and native
fur traders, within a few years the parents of most metis
children were both also metis. the basis of metis society
at this time was probably their unique economic position.
they acted as a kind of 'working class' for the hudson's bay
and northwest companies. they carried out work as provi-
sioners, transporters, clerks, and sometimes higher rank-
ing officials within the fur trading company. the metis
gained fame as buffalo hunters in the last half of the nineteenth century. they were also useful as interpreters, since
they often knew both a native and a non-native language.
interestingly, this was a role they often performed during
treaty negotiations.

the metis also developed their own language at this
time. their language is called 'michif,' and contains ele-
ments of aboriginal languages (cree, chipewyan, anishinabwe) and non-native languages (english, french, gaelic),
as well as terms and structures they invented. for these
reasons – their distinctive social and economic position
as well as their distinctive language – the metis are best
understood as a unique culture. metis often like to argue
that they try to bring together the best of both aboriginal and non-native cultures, and that they act as a sort

of bridge between two worlds. it is clear that they also became more than just a combination. they became a new people with a new culture.

the high point, historically, for metis society was the nineteenth century. the metis had not only a society but a land base. their first communities were focused on the red river settlements, around present-day winnipeg. later they spread to the north and west, especially through what is now northern saskatchewan and alberta and into the nwt. there are many good books available on the metis. one, called *the new people*, edited by jennifer brown and jacquelin peterson, contains a variety of essays that look at early metis society and culture. maria campbell's *half breed* is also a classic in the field.

the rupertsland purchase

the first riel rebellion was as much a constitutional crisis as it was a rebellion. there was relatively little force involved and eventually the situation was resolved through negotiations.

in the middle of the 1800s, the hudson's bay company was bought by a group of bankers who were less interested in the fur trade than they were in the mining potential of rupertsland. when canada formed in 1867, the hbc was prepared to sell their title to rupertsland in exchange for money to help them explore for minerals. canada, which then consisted of ontario, quebec, and some maritime provinces, was interested in expanding its control into the northwest.

so, in the late 1860s, canada and the hbc negotiated the sale of the northwest, known as the rupertsland purchase. this would eventually lead to the signing of the numbered treaties, which i discussed earlier. its more immediate result was the first riel rebellion.

the year 1868 had been very bad for both the selkirk settlers and the metis in the red river area. the buffalo hunt had failed for the metis, a sign of future problems with the buffalo. locusts had ruined the crops of both the metis and the settlers. to make matters worse, even the fisheries had failed. these failures led to many families' going hungry. by the next year, the metis were in no mood to be taken advantage of. in the late summer of 1869, canadian surveyors wandering over metis property only aggravated the situation. the metis knew about the rupertsland purchase, which was supposed to take effect on november 30, 1869. they knew that canada wanted to appoint a governor and council to rule the area. the metis were tired of being run by governors appointed by the hbc. they did not want to be run by new governors appointed by ottawa. they wanted a say in how things were run and in who ran them. so, they began to get in the way of the surveyors.

on october 16, 1869, the national committee of the metis was formed, with john bruce as president and louis riel as secretary. they set up a blockade of the pembina trail from the south on october 21. meanwhile, canada's appointed governor mcdougall was travelling with his family and council through the united states on the way to his new job. he was in for a big surprise. on november 2, when mcdougall reached st. norbert on the pembina trail, he was met by a group of armed metis who told him he was not welcome and turned him back. the same day, riel and 120 men took control of fort garry from the hbc. the metis then formed a provisional government until they could hold elections. mcdougall was forced to cool his heels on the american side of the border. his orders said he was supposed to take control on december 1, 1869. so, sometime between midnight and 4 a.m. that morning, he crept across the border, ponderously read his proclamation declaring rupertsland a part of canada, nailed it to a fencepost for the curious cows to read, and then turned tail back to the safety of the us.

the metis, who had real control of the red river area, prepared their demands in a 'list of rights' and a 'declaration of the people of rupertsland.' they were prepared to

negotiate *as equals*. in january 1870, ottawa sent a negotiating team. red river was too far away and the canadian
pacific railway did not yet exist, so it was impossible for
canada to easily or quickly send troops.

on february 10, the provisional government, led by
louis riel, officially took power and the national council
of the metis dissolved. a week later, thomas scott, one of
many orangemen in the red river area who opposed the
metis, was arrested outside fort garry with about fifty other
men. most of the men were released when they signed a
form saying they would not cause trouble. scott refused
to sign and continually harrassed his prison guards. on
march 3, he was tried before a metis council of war. riel
argued against punishing scott, but he was not listened
to. on march 4 scott was executed. this created hostility
towards the metis from ontario, where the media made a
hero out of a drunk – scott, and a demon out of a nation
builder – riel.

meanwhile, negotiations continued. on april 25
prime minister macdonald met with delegates from the
provisional government. they soon reached an agreement,
which included protection for metis land and cultural
rights but did not include an amnesty for metis activists.
on may 12, the *manitoba act* was passed by the federal government, including section 31, which read, "and whereas
it is expedient, towards the extinguishment of the indian

title to the lands in the province, to appropriate ... one million four hundred thousand acres [of land] for the families of the half-breed residents...."

legally, the metis won this rebellion. they got most of what they wanted. practically, though, things did not work out that way. near the end of may, colonel wolseley and his soldiers left toronto to take control. they reached fort garry in late august, carrying a warrent of arrest for riel, who had to flee.

the easterners were angry at having been beaten, so they went out of their way to make life difficult for the metis. although the metis had legal rights, general wolseley's troops and other eastern orangemen swaggered around, trampling over metis property and beating up any unprotected metis they could find. they acted like a conquering army, perhaps to compensate for the fact that they were whimpering thugs, the usual bearers of modernization, progress, and civilization.

many metis did not wait for their land – it would be a long wait, ten years before most land was given out – but left the area in search of peace and buffalo. this would eventually lead to the next riel rebellion. there are many books on the red river rebellion. try bruce sealy and antoine lussier's *the metis: canada's forgotten people* or gerald friesen's *the canadian prairies.*

batoche

things calmed down in the prairies for a while after the riel rebellion in manitoba. the first seven of the numbered treaties were negotiated between 1870 and 1877. the northwest territories, which at that time included present-day alberta, saskatchewan, and northern manitoba, as well as the nwt and yukon, was governed by a council controlled by the federal government.

the canadian pacific railway was being built and there was a lot of land speculation going on in western canada. this was creating the same kind of uncertainty for the metis that canadian surveyors had caused in 1869. through the 1870s, prime minister john a. macdonald continually rejected attempts by the metis of the nwt to have their title to land recognized. by the early 1880s, the metis were upset enough to start getting seriously organized. in the spring of 1884, they sent a delegation, led by the wily buffalo hunter, gabriel dumont, down to montana to try to convince louis riel to return. they hoped riel could lead them to the same sort of negotiated success that he had achieved in manitoba.

on june 5, 1884, riel and his family reached batoche, a metis centre, and a few days later, he made his first public speech there. all sorts of rumours began circulating about conspiracies and plans to join the us. in late august riel met with chief mistahimaskwa to promote support between indians and metis. the metis organized themselves into an official union and drafted a 'petition of rights,' similar to the one riel had used in manitoba, which they forwarded to ottawa. but things had changed since riel's success in 1869. the railway being built, could be used to move troops to the west more quickly. macdonald was not interested in negotiating so much as stalling for time. in fact, some historians believe that his cold responses to the metis were calculated to promote a rebellion, which would prove the value of a railway and help generate public support for increased government financing for the railway, which was nearly bankrupt.

while stalling the metis with the promise of a land commission, macdonald was also preparing an armed response. in march of 1885, the northwest mounted police (nwmp) at battleford, under the command of crozier, were reinforced with four officers and eighty-six horsemen. through march, events began to spin out of control. the rumour mill kept circulating and, on march 17, there was near panic in batoche over an unfounded rumour that the nwmp were on their way. on march 19, the metis declared that a provisional government had been formed and was in control of the northwest.

on march 26, at duck lake, saskatchewan, the first shots were fired. crozier and his 177 men approached the small community, where they met gabriel dumont and twenty-eight metis. crozier and 'gentleman' joe mckay (though he was no gentleman!) rode under a white flag and met isidore dumont (gabriel's brother) and asyiwin, a cree, in a field between the groups. the events of this meeting are not completely known, but the following seems most likely. all the men were on horse. gentleman joe had his rifle pointed towards dumont. dumont took exeception to this, and roughly shoved the point of the barrel away. gentleman joe then shot asyiwin dead, who became the first casualty of the rebellion. isidore dumont had no time to pull out his weapon, and was also shot.

seeing this, the metis attacked and quickly routed the nwmp, even though the metis were badly outnumbered. although they could have chased crozier and his men, riel prevailed on gabriel dumont (who was unaware that his brother had been killed earlier) not to press the attack. riel was probably hoping to be able to avoid more violence, so as to be in a better position to negotiate.

two days later, on march 28, general middleton and about 1000 troops arrived at que'appelle. on march 30, after it was far too late, the government finally appointed a commission to look into metis concerns. middleton already had his instructions to put down the insurrection.

prairie battles, prairie deaths

the frog lake killings took place a few days later. a group of mistahimaskwa's cree supporters had been celebrating 'big lies day' on april 1. led by a cree named wandering spirit, in the early hours of the morning of april 2, armed warriors gathered all the adult white men of the community together. according to my friend and colleague, the historian jarvis brownlie: "mistahimuskwa had been out hunting and had only just returned to the camp; in the meantime, wandering spirit had partly usurped the leadership role, and he was strongly anti-government and in favour of a more proactive approach to dealing with government abuse. the winter had been one of the coldest on record and the plains cree had suffered terribly, short of food, clothing, ammunition, and game (the game was depleted, and there were too many first nations people concentrated in a small area). the people remaining in mistahimuskwa's band were mostly those who were most defiant of government, since the others had drifted away earlier to join bands that were under treaty and therefore receiving food rations. it was spring, still a season of want, mistahimuskwa's people had endured a winter of suffering, and the local Indian agent, tom quinn, was hard-hearted if not sadistic in denying them food rations that were simply lying around in the storehouse. quinn had also physically mistreated a number of the men in the camp and had had one man imprisoned on a false charge in order to sleep with his wife. in short, he was abusive, cruel and incompetent and was slated to be transferred. moreover, the young cree men found it hard to endure the powerlessness and daily humiliations to which they were subjected by government agents, and their attitude was probably essentially 'better to die on our feet than live on our knees.'" as the warriors were taking their prisoners from one building to the next, one of the men, tom quinn, refused to obey an order. he was shot by wandering spirit and then eight other men, mostly priests and hbc staff, were killed. mistahimaskwa's role in this had been to urge his men not to kill or steal.

there were a few other battles and skirmishes that took place in the next month. among them were the battles of fish creek on april 24 and cut knife hill. on may 1, colonel otter and his soldiers came across poundmaker's camp. poundmaker hadn't chosen sides in the conflict but, on hearing that the army had attacked elders, women, and children, he fought to protect his people. while he could easily have destroyed otter's troops, he let them escape.

slowly, the forces began to gather at the metis centre of batoche. there are many good books on the second riel rebellion. try bob beal and rob macleod's *prairie fire,* or, another classic, howard adam's *prison of grass,* or the more recent *loyal till death* by bill waiser and blair stonechild.

the canadian navy and the battle of batoche

the battle of batoche, which lasted from may 9 to 12, 1885, was one of the most important events in metis and in western canadian history. on the government side were about 850 men led by general middleton, well armed, with the newly invented gattling gun and the steamer *northcote* providing support. on the metis side were less than 300 men led by gabriel dumont and louis riel. the metis were poorly armed, but they were more determined. they had also shown in the battle at fish creek that even with few numbers, they were quite capable of inflicting damage.

on may 9, the *northcote* won the distinction of becoming the first canadian navy vessel to see action. a group of soldiers tried to use the ship to establish a post downstream of batoche. the metis had set a trap. they strung a heavy rope across the high banks of the saskatchewan river, which snagged the *northcote*'s smokestack. they then easily disabled the ship with sniper fire from the shore.

most of the battle consisted in the soldiers on either side making occassional forays to try to establish a stronger position or in sporadic sniper fire. the metis were based in the scattered houses of batoche and in a trench line they had built up just outside town. the women and children and other non-combatants stayed in the church. middleton's troops were camped outside the town, near the banks of the river. they fought from trenches in positions nearer to the town. the fighting continued through may 10 and 11 with no outcome. notes were exchanged by both sides on various issues. for example, middleton was informed of the presence of non-combatants in the church and avoided directing fire in that direction. the metis quickly ran out of ammunition. they were using nails, stones, and anything else they could find in the older muskets but had trouble keeping even that kind of firepower going.

the final assualt

on may 12, middleton had ordered his troops not to make any all-out charges of the metis position. in spite of that order, an eager young colonel named arthur williams saw an opportunity early in the day and, without waiting for confirmation, led an attack. the metis soldiers, out of ammunition, were forced to retreat. they were routed and williams captured batoche. the battle was over. most of the metis, including riel and dumont, escaped.

on may 13, dumont left canada for the united states, where he received a hero's welcome. on may 15, riel surrendered, although he could have escaped. he was eventually hanged in the early morning of november 16, 1885. there is an interesting graphic comic biography of riel, called *louis riel* by chester brown. on may 26, 150 metis surrendered at battleford, thus ending the second riel rebellion. mistahimaskwa and poundmaker continued to fend off middleton's troops, but mistahimaskwa was forced to surrender on july 1. historians debate whether middleton was a crafty veteran who was avoiding bloodshed by waiting for the metis to run out of ammunition or a dithering coward who didn't want to fight.

historians also debate issues concerning the metis strategy. clearly, the metis military leadership was inspired. should the metis have tried to defend batoche, or, instead, stayed with successful guerrila warfare tactics? why was any bloodshed necessary, since metis demands were so moderate?

you can visit batoche today. it is a national historic site and there is a museum with presentations. you can walk over the battlefield and enjoy the view of the saskatchewan, or see the remains of the trenches or even some bullet holes! a good collection of essays on the aftermath of the 1885 resistance is *1885 and after*, edited by f.l. barron and james waldram.

history is carried by bodies: gabriel dumont

george woodcock wrote a biography of gabriel dumont called *gabriel dumont.* he was born around 1837 at st. boniface, part of the red river settlement. both his parents, isadore and louise, were metis. the dumonts were a prominent metis family; isadore was a leader of the great buffalo hunts. soon after gabriel was born, his family moved northwest, part of a general migration of the metis in search of better hunting grounds. he grew up in the vicinity of fort pitt. although he had no formal education and could not read or write, gabriel was well trained in the ways of the prairie. by the age of ten he could ride and even break horses. he became an excellent marksman. he learned six indigenous languages as well as french, though he never learned much english.

in 1858 gabriel married madelaine wilkie; they did not have any children. he was a part of the group led by his father and brother that negotiated peace between the metis and the dakota souix in 1862. a year later, gabriel, in his mid-twenties, was elected leader of the saskatchewan buffalo hunt. however, when it became clear that hunting alone was not enough to keep a family going, gabriel staked out land in 1872 near st. laurent, a mission community. he continued to lead the buffalo hunt, but also relied on farming and a small store and ferry service.

gabriel was relatively prosperous, generous, and well liked. he was elected president of the st. laurent community council when it was established in 1873, and re-elected the next year. one of the council's rules was that all hunters had to join the main buffalo hunt party, rather than hunt on their own, in order to co-ordinate activities. in the summer of 1875, gabriel made headlines in eastern canada by enforcing the rule over the protest of an independent, english-canadian-led hunt. because the st. laurent council was not recognized by the government, they put a warrant out to arrest gabriel dumont. but, realizing that it would be a mistake to harm such a prominent member of the community, they let him off with a warning.

in the next ten years, the metis tried to get the canadian government to recognize their land rights as the buffalo hunt grew less successful. the last major hunt, led by dumont, of the st. laurent metis took place in the early 1880s. dumont was not at the forefront of the frustrating political negotiations in these years because he had no inclination for written petitions. along with others, he recognized that negotiations were getting nowhere, and advocated trying to do what had been done in manitoba in 1870. in the spring of 1884, dumont was part of a group that travelled to montana and successfully convinced riel to rejoin his people as leader.

the next year was the year of the second riel rebellion, centred on batoche. riel led the metis, with dumont as the military leader. gabriel's military leadership was impressive; he was outnumbered and had to struggle against riel's poor judgment. it is also worth noting that at the first battle, duck lake, he received a painful wound in the head; he was a military leader who constantly exposed himself to danger.

gabriel easily escaped the patrols that searched for him after the metis defeat at batoche, and wound his way down to montana. his wife, madelaine, joined him there but died in 1886. dumont tried to organize a rescue of riel, but the task was impossible. for a few months in 1886 he worked with buffalo bill's wild west show, telling stories of the rebellion and demonstrating his marksmanship. he then lived in new york and, in 1888, after the canadian government granted an amnesty to the metis rebels, he moved to quebec.

finally, in 1890, dumont moved back to saskatchewan, travelling around batoche, red river, and montana. in 1891, late one night, an assassin tried to knife him but he fought the assassin off. dumont regained title to his old piece of land, but preferred to live with a nephew, doing a bit of hunting and fishing and telling stories of the old days. he remained a strong, active man in his old age and died on may 19, 1906. gabriel, gabriel, where are you now?

red indians: the league of indians

the first serious attempt to create a national political organization for native people took place in 1919 with the founding of the league of indians. provincial organizations, like the allied tribes of bc and the grand general indian council of ontario and quebec, had already been in existence for some time.

the league of indians was started by mohawks who opposed the *oliver act*, legislation to enfranchise indians who were returned world war one veterans. a founding convention, attended by as many as 1500 indians, was held in sault ste. marie in 1919 and fred ogilvie loft was chosen as leader. f.o. loft, as he signed his circulars, was a veteran who had probably lied about his age (he was too old) in order to volunteer. a mohawk, he was in his late fifties when he became leader of the league. he made his living as an accountant.

after he was elected, loft sent a letter or circular to most of the band councils in the country, saying that it was unfortunate that indians "were strangers to each other" because their problems were so similar. writing that "we should be treated as men and not imbeciles," loft called for more self-determination, recognition of aboriginal rights to hunt, fish, and trap, and a secure land base.

loft's circulars seemed to strike a chord among other indian leaders. over the next few years, well-attended

conventions of the league were held in manitoba, saskatchewan, and alberta. an indian agent wrote to the
department that indians on 'his' reserve were getting
"quite worked up about letters they received from someone named loftus or loftee." rather than encouraging the
league as a representative voice of indians that could help
the department consult with native people about what
decisions should be made, government immediately took
a hostile position.

the superintendent general of indian affairs at the
time, duncan campbell scott, seemed to have a personal
dislike for loft and recommended to his staff that they
"snub him." he also wrote that "it would seem essential
that the department should as far as possible curb or at
least keep informed as to loft's activities." the department
began to take a more active role in curbing loft's activities. they made sure the rcmp was in position to attend
and monitor the league's conventions. they also formally
refused to recognize loft as a legal representative of indians, and would not allow him to carry forward their grievances. in 1927 the department sponsored an amendment
to the *indian act,* preventing anyone from collecting dues
in order to fight on behalf of indians.

when the department refused to recognize loft, he was
forced to go around the bureaucrats. he went to the politicians and to the media, generating some of the first seriously

bad publicity for indian affairs. for example, in the *toronto star,* he was quoted as saying the department took a "dictatorial and domineering" approach towards indians.

while the 1927 amendment was being passed, loft was in chicago attending to his dying wife. when he returned, he found that his organization had effectively been outlawed. by this time he was in his late sixties. in spite of the ban, loft tried to raise money to go to england and mount a legal challenge to provincial hunting laws. the department gathered a file on loft and prepared to prosecute him, but he died before they could throw him in jail.

loft's legacy is generally intangible. the league of indians never developed into a full-fledged national organization and, especially in eastern canada, depended too much on loft himself. he did inspire the next generation of aboriginal leaders and, in the west, a spin-off from loft's organization, called the western league of indians, continued and thrived through the 1930s. loft also found ways of using the politicians and the media to get what he wanted when the bureaucrats were too obstructive. these tactics would be followed decades later by his successors.

for many indian bands across the country, the league gave them a chance to say 'no' to their indian agents and begin to fight back. its existence pointed to a deep discontent that would surface in the following decades. the league of indians and f.o. loft still have not been given the book-length study their story deserves. e. brian titley's biography of d.c. scott, *a narrow vision*, includes a chapter on loft, as does norma sluman's biography of cree leader *john tootoosis*. i've written an article on loft called "a considerable unrest" in the *native studies review*, 1988.

the theft of paradise did not go unopposed

the history of organized aboriginal political struggle in bc is among the oldest in the country. the bc indians, who had a rich heritage of diplomacy, began in the late nineteenth century to agitate for treaties or land claims. for example, at a royal commission to examine the question in 1888, david mackay, who spoke for the nisga'a, said "what we don't like about the government is their saying this: 'we will give you this much land.' how can they give it when it is our own? we cannot understand it." the nisga'a were among the most prominent to lead this fight for land rights. in 1908 they formed a nishga land committee, which took a petition for their land to the privy council office in london in 1913. the petition failed.

at a second royal commission on the land issue, in 1915, gideon minesque spoke for the nisga'a, saying, a "white man said that they must be dreaming when they say they own the land upon which they live. it is not a dream – we are certain that this land belongs to us." as you can see, over the years the nisga'a have had many eloquent spokespeople. partly to show support for the nisga'a, since the land question affected everyone, a broader based organization, called the allied tribes of british columbia, was formed in 1916. intense lobbying and organization took place in this period. b.c indians tended to be divided along a line that separated southern, interior indians from northern, coastal indians. the coastal indians had an advantage in becoming politically organized because boat travel made it easy for them to communicate with each other.

in 1921, the privy council in london, which then functioned as canada's supreme court, decided a case in southern nigeria that showed a clear tendency towards the recognition of aboriginal title. had the nisga'a pursued their legal claim at this time, and gone to the privy council relying on this precedent, they might have won their case. paul tennant's book, *aboriginal peoples and politics,* argues that, partly in response to a fear that this might take place, the *indian act* amendment in 1927 to ban the collecting of dues for the processing of indian grievances was directed against the allied tribes.

when in doubt, ban it!

one of the most notorious actions the government of canada took in the administration of indian affairs was an amendment to the *indian act* that banned the collecting of dues for political purposes. in 1927 the *indian act* was changed so that any person who tried to raise money for indian causes could be fined or imprisoned.

the actual language of section 141 of the 1927 *indian act* read: "every person who … receives, obtains, solicits or requests from any indian any payment or contribution … for the purpose of raising a fund or providing money for the prosecution of any claim which the tribe or band of indians to which such indian belongs, … has or is represented to have for the recovery of any claim or money for the benefit of the said tribe or band, shall be guilty of an offence." in arguing for this section of the *indian act,* the administors and politicians at the time constantly referred to outside 'agitators' and 'lawyers' who might be trying to take advantage of indians. for example, while responding to a complaint about the application of the ban, duncan campbell scott wrote that "i may say that this section was passed in order to protect the indians, particularly those of the more primitive type such as are found at barriere from exploitation from unscrupulous persons." at the time, scott was the deputy-superintendent general of indian affairs. the indians at barriere probably could have used some 'protection' from scott and his paternalistic approach! it is clear that by this time, the policy of protection, adopted formally since the *royal proclamation of 1763*, was being distorted completely out of shape.

protection, by 1927, had come to justify control. instead of implying a policy of secure land ownership for native peoples, protection had come to mean, for the government, knowing more than native peoples about what was in their best interests. this in turn justified interference in many aspects of native peoples' lives, including a curtailing of basic civil liberties. it is clear that lawyers and outside agitators were not the real targets of section 141 of the 1927 *indian act*. aboriginal leaders like fred loft were the targets. both the league of indians and the allied tribes of british columbia were strong and growing, and the department did not want its power challenged by them.

scott had always been concerned about the league of indians and had tried to discredit it by suggesting it was just a scheme for fred loft, a way of raising money. there was also concern that, in light of the privy council's legal decision on the southern nigeria case of 1921, the nisga'a land claim could be successful if taken through the courts.

the disolution of the allied tribes of bc may have been a direct result of section 141. certainly the section made things harder on the league of indians. the department was preparing to prosecute loft in 1931, but did not proceed, due to his untimely death. there seem to have been very few arrests or prosecutions made under this section. an american indian, clinton rickard, was charged under the section in 1931. in 1935 the department considered charging albert thompson, a manitoba indian, but did not. nevertheless, the amendment should be seen as an important part of indian history. the ban on collecting dues for political purposes was not lifted until 1951. so, for a quarter of a century, aboriginal people were denied the basic political right of assembly and organization.

instead of encouraging aboriginal people to speak for themselves and take control of their lives, indian affairs deliberately used the *indian act* as a legal tool to discourage those activities. today, when we criticize aboriginal organizations for relying on government grants and biting the hand that feeds them, we would do well to remember who did the biting first! there are two good reports from the treaties and historical research center of indian and northern affairs that deal with the 1927 amendment. one is called *the historical development of the indian act*, edited by john leslie and ron maguire. the other is *canadian indian policy during the inter-war years* by john leonard taylor.

history is carried by bodies: andrew paull

andrew paull's career bridges the gap between the efforts of those like f. o. loft in the 1920s and george manuel and his generation in the 1960s and 1970s to organize a national native political voice. paull was politically active from the 1920s through to the 1950s. you can read about andrew paull in an article by e. palmer patterson ii, which has been reprinted in a book called *one century later*, edited by ian a.l. getty and donald b. smith. he is also discussed in george manuel and michael poslun's *the fourth world*.

born in 1892 on the squamish reserve, near what today is north vancouver, paull was educated and heavily influenced by roman catholics. his grandmother and other community elders helped to teach paull in the ways of his people. he believed he had gained both an 'indian education' and a 'european education.' paull seems to have been one of those people who was a natural organizer and was gifted with a lot of energy. as well as politics, he was active in sports. he wrote sports columns for vancouver newspapers and organized baseball, lacrosse and boxing events. he played musical instruments and organized an orchestra. he was also active in the longshoreman's union in vancouver when he worked as a longshoreman, and organized an employment service for indians. rolf knight's great book, *indians at work*, deals with the history of indigenous people and the labour movement in bc.

the development of the allied tribes of british columbia gave a young andrew paull a place where his talents could flourish. with peter kelly, he became a leading figure in the allied tribes until its demise after the 1927 revisions to the *indian act*. one of his main jobs was to help present the land claims of bc indians to a special joint committee of the senate and house of commons in 1927.

the next major wave of activity for paull, after the allied tribes, was a two-year job as office manager of the native brotherhood of british columbia (nbbc), beginning in 1942. paull helped that organization, which was mainly concerned with economic matters, to spread its influence into the south of bc. a disagreement over the extent of his authority led paull to resign from the nbbc, but he soon was helping to form an organization called the north american indian brotherhood (naib) in ottawa in 1944. it would become paull's vehicle and he its leading spokesperson. paull became its president a year later.

the naib attempted to act as a national 'commonwealth' of indian nations, and provide a national or even international voice for aboriginal peoples. paull helped pressure the government after world war two to set up a special committee to revise the *indian act*. paull appeared before the committee, arguing for a resolution of bc land claims and raising the question of indian citizenship. he did not hesitate to be critical of government and of the committee itself, and helped to generate some of the first public criticism the committee faced for not having any native representation.

although the naib had the support of many leaders and the energy of andrew paull, it never firmly established itself and never had the necessary support from local aboriginal political organizations. when andrew paull died in 1959, the naib lost most of its influence, although it continued for another decade. paull was a tireless organizer who inspired later leaders, including george manuel, who would go on to be one of the first leaders of the national indian brotherhood. as patterson ii has written, "in the development of indian responsibility for their own affairs, andrew paull exerted a constant and lasting influence."

a few thoughts concerning the 1951 indian act

it is my view that the changes made to the *indian act* in 1951 represented a significant shift in canadian indian policy. not a shift in the ultimate goal of that policy, which was still assimilation, but, rather, a shift in the way the government tried to achieve that goal. most scholars disagree with my assessment, finding, as john l. tobias wrote, "there are only minor differences" between the *indian act* of 1876 and that of 1951. james s. frideres, another respected scholar, wrote that the two acts were "depressingly similar." i want to present a different point of view.

in addition to this particular debate, it is worthwhile looking at the 1951 *indian act* because it is basically the act that is with us today. *bill c-31*, in 1985, was the only really major change to the *indian act* since 1951. the only book-length treatment of the 1951 *indian act* comes from the treaties and historical research centre of diand. it is called *helping indians help themselves: the 1951 indian act consultation process* by ian v.b. johnson.

there are four main reasons why the government found it necessary to change the *indian act* after world war two. firstly, many non-native canadians in church groups and other organizations had become concerned about native people's civil rights. after the war, which was perceived to be a war against racism, they put pressure on the government to do something about civil rights. secondly, it became clear that many of the assumptions behind indian policy were untrue. by the 1940s, it was easier to see that indians would not be a 'vanishing race.' the status indian population was actually growing, not decreasing, and that meant that enfranchisement was not working. thirdly, indians had made a very strong contribution to the war effort. their buddies, who relied on them in war, did not like the second-class treatment indians received when they returned home. veterans' groups lobbied for changes, and indian soldiers who gained skills in the army also argued for change. finally, indian political organizations had grown strong enough to begin to have some influence. their fight for change finally started to make inroads in the post-war climate. the last three reasons seem to me to be the most important in this list. in various ways, the indian struggle for change, resistance to assimilation, and contribution to canadian society forced the government to rethink its approach.

the committee to examine itself...

many indian and non-indian groups called on the government to set up a royal commission on aboriginal affairs. the government bowed to the pressure as little as possible and, instead, in 1946 set up a special joint committee of the senate and house of commons to make recommendations about revising the *indian act.* it held hearings between 1946 and 48. its terms of reference were narrow, and basically kept it focussed on the *indian act* and administration. there were no native people on the committee.

   although the committee was set up because of the pressure that had been put on the government to make some positive changes, the members of the committee were not well informed about indian issues. they did not understand the idea of aboriginal rights. for example, d.f. brown, one of the co-chairs of the committee, said, "i believe it is a purpose of this committee to recommend actually some means whereby indians have rights and obligations equal to those of all other canadians. there should be no difference in my mind, or anybody else's mind, as to what we are, because we are all canadians." most of the witnesses called by the committee were bureaucrats who worked for indian affairs. some of these people had outright racist attitudes. a major mackay, who was the indian commissioner of bc, testified before the committee that "an indian requires constant attention and supervision. it does not do to suggest certain things to them and leave it at that."

because the committee spent so much time listening to officials from indian affairs, indian leaders at the time called it a "committee to investigate itself." one part of government was talking to another part of government about indians, but indians themselves had no say. diamond jenness, the famous anthropologist, spoke to the committee. he presented a "plan for liquidating canada's indian problem within 25 years." the committee was enthusiastic about this plan, but in the end did not adopt jenness's suggestions.

on june 27, 1946, andrew paull spoke to the committee. he was not happy with the way things were going and said, "i might as well warn you that i am going to say a few disagreeable things, so you might as well be prepared." paull proceeded to condemn the committee, noting that its terms of reference were too narrow. he called for a royal commission and for the committee to disband itself. he attacked the *indian act* and indian affairs and called for more self-government.

paull also said that if the committee did not dissolve itself, it should at least have more indian participation. this led to the first bad publicity for the committee when one of its members moved to allow indian leaders to join it and the motion was defeated.

in spite of the committee's reluctance to encourage indian participation, indians slowly forced themselves on to the agenda. indian bands from across the country mailed in hundreds of submissions calling for more self-government and changes to the *indian act*. in the last half of 1947, the committee was forced to hear indian leaders, such as like john calihoo of the indian association of alberta and a wide variety of other indian leaders from across the country. these leaders had strong views and many recommendations, including technical changes to the *indian act* and broad changes in the goals of indian policy. slowly, at a glacial pace, the canadian state and the newcomer society were forced to provide a forum for the voices of the indigenous people whose lands they occupied.

microscopic steps toward self-government

this special joint committee of the senate and the house released a number of official reports in the next few years. although the committee never went so far as to question the ultimate goal of indian policy, which at the time was assimilation, it did question the way the government was trying to achieve that goal. many of the committee's recommendations had to do with the organization of the indian affairs department and general administrative matters. however, in its later reports, the recommendations became more political in nature. for example, in response to intense pressure from aboriginal leaders to do something about land rights, the committee recommended setting up a land claims commission to deal with land-related grievances. they also recommended strengthening the protective measures embodied in the *indian act*, which had been weakened by successive governments since the turn of the century.

the most interesting recommendations, however, had to do with self-government. the committee wanted to encourage bands to have more self-government so they recommended that bands have more financial control. they also tried to limit the discretionary powers of the superintendent general of indian affairs. the committee thought that status indians should have the right to vote in federal elections and that indian women should have the right to vote for band councils. it made many other recommendations on both trivial and far-reaching matters.

the committee's work was supposed to lead to a revision of the *indian act*. however, in june of 1950, when the government proposed a new *indian act*, much to everyone's surprise they almost completely ignored the recommendations of their own committee! thus, the reports of the special joint committee became the first in a long series of reports the government would pay to have done and then largely ignore. it was followed by the hawthorn (1966), berger (1977), penner (1983), and coolican (1985) reports, and, perhaps most famously of all, by the royal commission on aboriginal peoples (1996): all commissioned by the government; all largely or completely ignored, though all did have far-reaching influence in educating the public.

because there had been so much publicity devoted to the committee of 1946 to 1948, critics embarrassed the government so much for ignoring its work that the *indian act* proposed in june of 1950 was withdrawn. instead, a new special committee was set up in april of 1951. it moved quickly to draft a new *indian act, bill c-179*, or the 1951 *indian act*.

the 1951 indian act: *from repression to ideology*

on may 17, 1951, a revised *indian act, bill c-179,* was passed in the house of commons. most of the changes that were made to the *indian act* after 1951 were small or minor ones. so, the 1951 *indian act* was the basis for the *indian act* we have today. the key assumption of the 1951 act was still assimilation. in that way, it was the same as the indian acts that came before it. the main difference was that, after 1951, the government tried to use a *different method* of assimilation.

one of the most important changes was that the new act got rid of the worst restrictions that had been placed on indians. the ban on the sundance and potlatch were removed, for example. also, after 1951, a pass signed by the indian agent was no long necessary for indians to travel off their reserves. the ban on collecting dues for political organizations was also dropped.

when you read about people comparing south african apartheid to canada's treatment of aboriginal people, it is important to keep these changes in mind. before 1951, the two systems were quite closely related, and south african politicians partly modelled the apartheid system on canada. however, after 1951, canada began to move away from a repressive regime while south africa grew increasing repressive towards its black majority. this does not mean colonization stopped in canada. rather, instead of using brute force as the main tool of assimilation, the government switched to 'soft power,' what some social scientists call 'ideology.' education and social intermingling, assimilating from the head down rather than from the body up, was to be the new approach.

the 1951 *indian act* also started to limit the discretionary powers of the department of indian affairs. this meant that the bureaucrats had less power because they controlled fewer areas. before 1951 the minister could initiate action in seventy-eight sections of the *indian act. bill c-179* gave the minister such power in only twenty-six clauses. so you could say that in a small way the act made some early advances towards aboriginal self-government.

one of the more complicated changes made by the 1951 *indian act* had to do with indian status. if you were enfranchised, you gained full status as a canadian. you could vote in elections but you lost your status as an indian. before 1951 the government could automatically enfranchise people whether or not they wanted to be enfranchised. for example, indians who became lawyers or doctors or who got a university degree were often automatically enfranchised.

after *bill c-179*, automatic enfranchisement for men was removed. the enfranchisement process stayed on the books, though, until 1985. involuntary enfranchisement for indian women was not changed; in fact, in some ways, it was made worse by the 1951 act. the act made many changes that affected indian women, as we shall see. hugh shewell's book on the history of first nations welfare, called *'enough to keep them alive,'* has a good account of this period, emphasizing the social situation.

and now, introducing the infamous section 12(1)(b).

section 6 of the first *indian act* (the *enfranchisement act* of 1869) discriminated against women, stating "that any indian woman marrying any other than an indian, shall cease to be an indian within the meaning of this act." this, and the process of enfranchisement itself, were what created the category 'non status indian.' many indian women lost their indian status, not by choice, but because the government took it away from them. however, they were still indians in terms of their bodies, their identities, and their lifestyles.

the question of indian women's status was looked at by the special joint committee of senate and house of commons in 1946. there had been considerable debate over what should happen, but there was not much support for removing the discriminatory clause. in fact, the 1951 *indian act* made the discrimination even worse by the addition of a new section, section 12 (1) (b), which made sure that any vestige of status, including status with the band and treaty rights, were also lost to native women who married non-natives. before then, it had been possible to lose indian status but keep status with the band and keep treaty rights. the new rules would remain in force until 1985.

there were some positive changes made for native women by the 1951 *indian act*. before then, they did not have the right to vote for band councils – only adult males could vote. but, after 1951, women could be formally involved in local political affairs and exercise voting powers.

all in all, the 1951 *indian act* signalled a change in the kinds of measures the government would use to achieve its goal of assimilating indians.

for these reasons, i think that the 1951 act was an important shift in indian policy and, in some ways, the first step in the long road to self-government. quite a lot has been written in recent years about discrimination against women in the *indian act. enough is enough: aboriginal women speak out*, by the women of tobique, as told to janet silman, is a good book, which explains the effects of the discrimination and the struggle to end it.

managing inuit: the post-war regime

in the period after world war two, inuit history made a major shift, largely because government policy in that period began to change. the federal government had to become more active in the canadian arctic for a number of reasons. as i noted earlier, in 1939, the supreme court of canada ruled that inuit were a responsibility of the federal government. also, as a result of the war, large numbers of american soldiers had gone to the canadian arctic. this worried the canadian government regarding its ownership or sovereignty over the north. if there were more americans than canadians 'up there,' why should the arctic islands be considered canadian possessions?

the increased presence of the government, in some ways, was long overdue. inuit had been having serious problems, which the government basically ignored or dealt with in a cursory manner. in fact, prime minister louis st. laurent is reported as saying that canada had managed its north in a state of "absent mindedness."

however, the increased government involvement in the arctic was a mixed blessing. while it meant that, slowly, there were more schools, better medical care, and better welfare services for the needy, it also meant interference in people's lives. many decisions would be made in the next few decades, with little or no consultation with inuit, that would have a significant impact on inuit lives. one of these has to do with where people live. historians have come to pay a lot of attention to this question, because it shows the problems with the government's arctic policies.

of course, the fact that permanent settlements were created at all meant a change for inuit, who were used to being nomadic. the government wanted settlements in places that were easy to reach and less expensive to service. in some cases, this meant encouraging inuit to leave their traditional territories. this reached the point where, in the late fifties and early sixties, the government seriously discussed relocating all inuit to special compounds in the south. although in the end this was never enforced, many inuit were taken to the south for medical reasons and not taken back to the north. two books on these topics, are: *the road to nunavut* by r. ruinn duffy, and *the northward expansion of canada* by morris zaslow.

the high arctic exiles

there has been a growing controversy over the government's creation of two particular communities in the high arctic: grise fiord and resolute bay. those communities were settled in 1953 by inuit from inukjuak and pond inlet. the inuit from inukjuak experienced many difficulties because they were not familiar with the high arctic environment, which was much colder and darker than their own. they were also separated from their families and could not return home.

there is increasing evidence that at least the timing and specific location of these moves had as much to do with the government's wish to protect its ownership of high arctic islands as it did with concern for inuit welfare. it seems that in the late forties and early fifties, inuit from greenland were crossing over to ellesmere island and hunting there. since they were the only people using ellesmere, canada's claim to the island could have been seen to be quite weak.

shelagh grant, a former colleague of mine at trent univesity, has written an article called "a case of compounded error," published in *northern perspectives*, in which she argues that government's desire to protect its ownership of arctic islands was a key factor in the decision to relocate inuit from inukjuak. the government maintains that inuit were moved because overpopulation of the inukjuak area led to overhunting. since there was not enough wildlife to support the growing population, some families were moved to uninhabited areas.

the historical evidence seems to show that a concern for welfare and a concern for sovereignty both played a role in the decision to move inuit to these northern communities. the evidence also indicates that the move was very poorly planned and executed. the inuit involved say that many of them agreed to the move only because the rcmp put a lot of pressure on them. although inuit from pond inlet were moved to assist the inukjuak inuit to become used to more northern conditions, it was a drastic change of life for the people of inukjuak. when the actual move took place in 1953, there was a last-minute change of plans: the boats could not get to a third high arctic location so one of three original planned northern communities was scrapped. furthermore, it was only when they arrived at grise fiord that inuit were told they would be split up: some of them would stay and some of them go on to resolute bay. from all accounts, the first few years were very hard. stories are told of resolute bay inuit having to scrounge in the garbage of the nearby military base in order to get enough food.

many of the inuit asked to be taken back home after the first year. they say they had been promised that they could return if they did not like it in the high arctic. however, instead of returning inuit when they asked, the government put pressure on them to stay and relocated more of their relatives from inukjuak up to resolute bay. although they pressed the government for years, it was not until the seventies that many of them could, at their own expense, return home. others, of course, eventually laid down roots in the new communities or were born there and so stayed. the issue has become controversial because the inuit asked the government for a formal apology and for compensation. the government was supposed to be acting in a trust-like manner towards the inuit, keeping inuit interests foremost in their approaches, but did not seem to do so in this case.

this is an area of hotly argued debate for historians. most academics seem to be siding with the inuit, but there are those who support the government's position. the government commissioned a consultant's report, called the hickling report, which exonerated the government. a later human rights commission report, the soberman report, said the government owed the inuit an apology. in addition to shelagh grant's article, an article by alan marcus, called "out in the cold," published in *polar record,* discusses the case and provides support for the notion that sovereignty was at least a factor. frank tester and myself wrote a book that deals with the case re: eskimos, arctic administration, the high arctic exiles, and other events of the post-war period, called *tammarniit [mistakes].*

dissident communities: lubicon lake cree

the treaty 8 commissioners in 1899 missed the lubicon lake cree. they were a more isolated band of hunters who were out on the land when the treaty commission was negotiating and registering treaty indians. for this reason, they did not get a reserve, and their troubles began. there is an article on the lubicon in boyce richardson's great collection of essays by aboriginal leaders and others, called *drumbeat.*

in 1930 the government discovered its oversight and realized that the lubicon lake people were entitled to the same rights as other treaty 8 first nations. there was no pressure to do something right away because no one was interested in the land. to non-natives, it was an isolated backwater. in 1940 the band was promised a reserve that was supposed to be sixty-five square kilometres in size, based on the band's population at that time. however, the war effort kept the government from fulfilling this promise and nothing was done.

after the war, the issue was dropped; no one remembered the promise that had been made and, since very little economic development took place, there was no pressure on lubicon lands so the band was not concerned about the lack of a treaty. all this changed during the seventies oil boom. oil development, especially after 1976, seriously damaged the lubicon cree's land base. cut lines and oil wells ignored trapping and hunting territory, heavy equipment frightened away the animals, and people began to realize that even the land their houses were built on was not secure. the lubicon lake cree began pressing the federal government for a reserve. however, because of the *natural resources transfer act* of 1930, the provincial government had authority over crown land in alberta. both the federal and provincial government recognized that the lubicon lake cree deserved a reserve.

the alberta government insisted, though, that the reserve be the same size as had been promised in 1940. membership in the band had grown significantly, so the band thought they were entitled to more land. the band also thought it was entitled to compensation for the injustice that had been done. while negotiations dragged on, the lubicon began to feel the environmental and social costs of development. more hunting and trapping territory was disrupted. the moose hunts began to fail. hunters and trappers found it harder to make a living off the land. the community experienced growing problems with family violence, suicide, and alcoholism. the government tried to divide the lubicon lake cree by saying only some of them were 'real' members of the band, while others were metis or non-status indians and did not deserve any land. the band decided to fight back. in the early eighties, they began what would become one of the most high-profile, community-based struggles in canada.

a world-class boycott

by the mid-eighties, it was clear that the sides were getting no closer to solving the problem, so an independent consultant was hired to analyze the situation and make compromise recommendations. the consultant was e. davie fulton, and in 1986 he drafted a report that generally sided with the lubicon. the government then basically ignored the report for which it had paid. the lubicon were forced to be increasingly creative in pressuring the governments to listen to their demands. much of this struggle took place outside the established structure for negotiating conflicts between first nations and the canadian state. by looking at it in historical perspective, we learn a lot about what is involved in trying to go outside the system.

in the fall of 1987 and winter of 1988, the lubicon generated a great deal of publicity and an international audience for their cause by sponsoring a boycott of the 1988 calgary winter olympics. they also boycotted the "spirit sings" exhibit of native culture at the glenbow museum. they said they couldn't understand how people could be celebrating native culture behind glass cases while trying to destroy it in real life. on october 15, 1988, the lubicon set up a blockade on the road that gave access to their traditional lands. they were prepared to give their own licences to companies that wanted to develop their lands, at a price. a week later, the rcmp arrested twenty-seven people who were at the blockade. however, the premier of alberta, don getty, met personally with bernard ominayak, the chief of the lubicon. the two arrived at a deal where the provincial government agreed to provide enough land for the current needs of the band.

things are still not easy for the lubicon lake cree. the federal government, which, before 1988, could blame the provincial government for the dispute, dragged its heels. it refused to pay a fair measure of compensation for damages that had been done to the lubicon community, it argued with the province over who should share what costs, and it sponsored the creation of a separate band to try to divide the community again.

so the lubicon continue to struggle, but they have taught all of us something about what it means to try to take power into your own hands. and they have taught us about what to do when the system says no. there is a book on the lubicon called *last stand of the lubicon lake cree* by john stoddard.

communities: teme-augama anishnabai

like the lubicon lake cree of northern alberta, the teme-augama anishnabai (people of the deep water) feel they were missed by the treaty commissioners. the two robinson treaties (huron and superior) were both negotiated in the year 1850 with ojibwe of northern ontario, but chief nebanegwune of the teme-augama anishnabai was not present at the treaty negotiations. the government maintains that the chief of a nearby band, chief tawgaiwene (spelled tagawinini in the treaty), was acting on behalf of the temagami band when he signed the treaty.

the band started asking the government for a reserve and for other treaty benefits, including annuities. in 1883 the federal government began paying the band treaty money every year, but did not set aside a reserve. finally, in 1943, the government of ontario transferred bear island on lake temagami to the federal government for use as a reserve. in 1971 bear island officially became a reserve. you can see how quickly the federal government moves to act for indigenous peoples.

this was not what the band had wanted. they needed more land than just one small island. they wanted their reserve to included traditional lands around the shore of their lake, and bear island was not large enough to support their people. there is a fairly comprehensive account of the historical background to temagami in a book by bruce hodgins and jamie benidickson, called *the temagami experience.*

the resulting struggles of the teme-augama anishna-bai to their homeland, which they call n'daki-menan, took many different forms, from blockades and civil disobedience to arguments in the courts.

in canada, it's called 'just-us'

in the summer of 1973, soon after the supreme court of canada made its famous ruling in the calder case about nisga'a land rights, the teme-augama band filed a land caution. they argued that they still had unsurrendered aboriginal title to their traditional territory. the caution was a legal tool that worked to prevent anyone from taking or developing this land until the question of title was sorted out. upset by this move, the ontario government tried to get the caution removed in 1978. the band and the provincial government then started to play legal football. the government sued the band in the supreme court of ontario, while the band continued to try to get the courts to affirm its title.

the key question in these court cases was whether the band had extinguished its title through the robinson treaty of 1850. in 1979 the band decided to stop taking treaty money, so that they could show that they did not see themselves as descendants of signatories to the treaty. after loosing the case, the band appealed, but the appeal court of ontario in 1979 decided that aboriginal title had been surrendered (or extinguished) in three ways: through the treaty, through the band's acceptance of treaty money, and because the government had clear intentions of extinguishing title. the appeal court was also not happy with the oral history presented during the trial because it came from chief potts rather than from other elders in the band, who would have been seen as direct sources. the band appealed this verdict to the supreme court of ontario. the case was heard there beginning in 1982. after 119 days in court, a decision was eventually handed down in december of 1984. the judge, justice steele, ruled that the band had extinguished its title through the treaty process, and went so far as to question whether the band had, in fact, occupied the land from time immemorial. one witness, an historian named charles bishop, had argued that the band had come together in the area as late as 1857, when a fur trade post was re-established on the lake. finally, in the early nineties, the supreme court of canada, the band's last chance, rejected their arguments and turned down the last appeal. the band had lost its case in the courts.

this case shows us that while there have been some important legal victories for aboriginal people through the courts in recent years, there have also been some significant losses. in this case the legal decisions that went against them may have been poor ones and could even be called racist in some respects, but that is cold comfort. the band, from its small reserve on bear island, has still managed to move forward on many fronts. it is fortunate that they used other tactics and did not rely solely on the courts.

n'daki-menan

as the legal battles began in the 1970s, the area, n'daki-menan ('homeland'), became contested, for similar reasons that we saw with the lubicon cree. the natural resources, this time the forests, became desirable to logging companies, but the temagami area had also come to be an important wilderness retreat for many non-natives from southern ontario, and a growing issue for environmentalists.

as the legal struggles were going nowhere, in may of 1988, the band decided by consensus that on june 1 they would blockade the access roads being constructed to lead into the old-growth areas. for the next few months, road construction continued in a climate of hostility. people on the blockade were frequently arrested and many charges were laid. bob rae, then leader of the opposition in the ontario government, joined the blockade for a few hours in the fall to demonstrate his support for the band. students and professors at a number of universities also supported the band on the blockades and by raising funds. in december, after six and a half months, the ontario court of appeal ordered a removal of the blockade *and* a halt to further road construction for the time being.

the blockade helped to make many people aware of the teme-augama anishnabai struggle. it brought together a wide range of people, natives and non-natives, concerned about logging in the area for many different reasons. although it did not prevent the access road from being built, it created enough political pressure that the provincial government was forced to revise its plans for development in the area. a joint management authority was eventually set up to develop long-term plans for the area, with the local anishnabai playing a prominent role. meanwhile, the band continued to press its claim for aboriginal title through the courts. chief gary potts of the teme-augama anishnabai has a very good chapter in *drumbeat*, edited by boyce richardson, on the struggle of his people.

dissident communities: nitassinan

"nitassinan" is what the innu people of northern quebec and labrador call their traditional homeland. the innu people are related to the cree and ojibwe, speaking a dialect of the same language, and are not related to the inuit of the arctic. in the past, these people were called montagnais or montagnais-naskapi. the word "innu" ("human beings" or "people") is their own word for themselves.

similar to the struggles of the lubicon and temiaugama anishnabai, there has been a growing struggle in nitassinan over how the land will be used. daniel ashini, a former innu chief, has a good article on his people's struggle in the book, *drumbeat.*

innu along the northern coast of the st. lawrence river may have been among the earliest of canada's first nations in the modern period to have encountered a european. in 1534, jacques cartier travelled along the coast of nitassinan. the innu from the southern part of their territory were heavily involved with the jesuits and the fur trade. they developed an economy that relied on travelling to the coast to trade furs and then back inland to hunt and trap. however, the innu remained among the most traditional of canada's first nations. their culture and values remained very strong into the twentieth century. in the fifties, the canadian government began to encourage the innu to settle in permanent villages. there they experienced many of the same problems other native communities found: poor housing, social problems, and a foreign education system. some innu refused to move until as late as the early seventies. many continue to rely on life on the land for a large part of their subsistence.

in 1927, without consulting the innu, great britain and canada carved their traditional territory in half. the eastern half became a part of newfoundland; the western half became a part of quebec. the innu depend upon caribou for much of their food. the caribou do not read maps very well, and ignore the border. so the innu have to ignore the border as well if they want to be able to hunt. but they can get charged and arrested for hunting in the wrong province if they cross the invisible line that divides their own traditional territory. but the worst was yet to come. nitassinan, the traditional homeland of the innu, was slowly to become a key link in the western world's military plans.

two four-letter words (innu and nato)

in 1942, as part of the war effort, an american air force base was built in goose bay, close to the innu community of sheshatshit. the population of the area virtually tripled overnight, with many people from labrador and new-foundland joining american soldiers in the community.

this base was used as a fueling stop for aircraft on their way overseas and had little effect further from the base. when the british began practising with their vulcan planes in the late fifties and sixties, there was greater impact, but still the planes didn't fly low enough to affect the innu hunters and trappers. all this changed in the 1980s when the british and the west germans began practice flights with supersonic fighters very close to the ground. in contrast to the heavily populated and restricted territories of west germany and england, nitassinan seemed like the perfect 'empty' wilderness for practising 'contour' flight training (flying under the enemy radar). canada encouraged the use of goose bay because it was an easy and cheap way for it to contribute to nato.

canada also thought that by expanding the base at goose bay, it was providing economic development to the region. if you've followed this history this far, you'll know by now that 'economic development' is a code phrase that translates into english as 'raping the land for the benefit of the rich.' it is still used all the time. no one thought about the people on the ground underneath the planes who had their own kind of economy, based on hunting and trapping. no one thought very much about what it was like to be underneath a jet fighter, weighing twenty to thirty tons, flying at 900 miles an hour only thirty metres above the ground.

in her book *nitassinan*, marie wadden notes that the noise from these jets can be measured at 110 to 140 decibles. a jackhammer is measured at 80 decibles, and 120 decibles can cause pain in humans, not to mention the startle effect, since these jets almost always come on people and caribou so quickly they catch them by surprise. and then there's the air and water polution. wadden's book pays particular attention to the role of innu women, like elizabeth peneshue, whom i met and by whom i was deeply inspired. at a meeting of the innu in may of 1985, they decided they had had enough. they wanted to stop the flights. but how?

innu resistance, from the ground up

the innu sent delegations over to europe to see if there was support for their struggle. they found environmental and peace groups who were willing to support them. they did not find the political leaders of european countries very helpful, though. in the mid-1980s, things began to look worse, with the number of flights increasing from 3,000 to 7,000 by 1988. in 1986 the canadian government signed an international agreement allowing the us, uk, west germany, and the netherlands to practise low-level flying in the region for ten years. the innu were not getting their message across using education and discussion. they were forced to take more drastic measures.

in the fall of 1987, a group of innu travelled from sheshatshit to a bombing range. the plane that took them could not fly over the range, so they were dropped off and had to hike in. they had been told that the military planes were dropping only very small test bombs. bart penashue, a young innu hunter and spokesperson, said, "some of these bombs weigh over a thousand pounds, and they make huge craters in the ground, one we saw was over seven feet deep." the group set up tents and kept a camp on the bombing range for ten days, forcing the military to close the range. the next fall, another camp was set up on the range. on september 15, a group of innu walked on the runway of the airbase. they were concerned because they had not been able to meet with a team of nato surveyors. nato was considering the area as the site of a possible major flight training centre. a meeting was quickly arranged and the innu were bused from the runway.

in the late eighties, nato was looking to build an $800 million tactical fighter weapons training centre in either turkey or canada. it would have involved a dramatic increase in the amount of low overflights, to over 40,000. the innu were determined to see that this base was not built on their homeland. on september 22, about a hundred innu again stormed the runway. this time they refused to leave and had to be carried or dragged off. they were charged. the same day the innu set up a peace camp just beyond the perimeter of the runway. this camp had between one and two hundred people staying at it, and lasted until mid-december. when they tried to set up the camp again in march of 1989, police kept them from the site, took apart their tents, and arrested some of them. by the end of march, twenty-six innu were in jail. in early april the trial of the innu involved in these disturbances began. in all, some 223 mischief charges were filed against the innu.

in canada, it may still be possible to find justice that is not just us

in goose bay on april 4, 1989, the trial of four innu leaders began. they were charged with mischief because they had gone on to the runway at the military base to try to prevent the jets from taking off. the jets had been frightening people in their hunting camps, scaring the caribou, and polluting the air and water.

the judge for the trial was an inuk, james igloliorte. (the word "inuk" is inuktitut, the inuit language, and means a "single inuit person.") he agreed to move the trial to a large hall nearer sheshatshit. the lawyer for the innu argued that, because the innu honestly believed that the land was theirs, they were legally justified in attempting to set up a camp on the runway. the trial went on for three days. on april 18, the judge gave his decision. he agreed with the innu arguments, saying "each of these four persons based their belief of ownership on reasonable grounds. through their knowledge of ancestry and kinship they have showed that none of their people ever gave away rights to the land to canada, and this is an honest belief each person holds." the innu were let off.

this victory gave the innu a great boost. they planned more protest marches, demonstrations, and sit-ins. a series of arrests and trials followed, with many of the innu and their supporters spending quite a lot of time in jail. the crown, meanwhile, had appealed igloliorte's decision. in october 1989, the newfoundland court of appeal nullified the trial and acquittal. however, the innu had succeeded in making their cause known around the world and in southern canada. in november 112 people were arrested in ottawa for protesting in front of the department of defense on behalf of the innu.

in november 1990, another protest was held in ottawa, as part of a "freedom for nitassinan" walk. i was at that protest, part of a crowd that tried to close down the department of defense building for a day and one of over a hundred people, including a small group of innu, who were charged. nato defense ministers announced in may, 1991, after months of delay, speculation, and worry, that the tactical fighter weapons training centre would not be built. this was a great relief to the innu and a great victory, but their struggle was not over.

low overflights continue over nitassinan. although the proposed base was not built, the number of over-flights continued to grow: from 7,000 flights a year in 1988 to 9,000 flights a year in 1990. so, the struggle of the innu goes on. they are still trying to get the overflights stopped, they have been in the news for blockading a log-ging road, and they are still trying to get their aboriginal title to traditional lands affirmed. meanwhile, the voisey's bay nickle find has come to trump most other concerns as the spectre of "economic development" rears its head again. and you know that that means, don't you?

the determination of the innu has shown that a small group of people can have an impact on even the most powerful interests in the western world. as well as the book and article about the innu i mentioned earlier, there is also a very good film by hugh brody, called *hunters and bombers*.

dissident communities: james bay cree

the james bay cree have been very successful at maintaining their traditional way of life. this is partly because their traditional territory is so far from southern capitals and partly because the fur trade was an economic activity that matched up well with subsistence activities.

well into the 1940s and 1950s, the james bay cree were living much as they had for centuries. they were affected by the bust and boom cycles of fur prices, but could still live on the land without much outside interference. this began to change in the fifties and sixties. by the late thirties, the government began appointing indian agents to each of the james bay cree communities. this started a process of government involvement that would grow larger and larger in the coming decades. official band councils were also set up and the provisions of the *indian act* were applied more consistently.

by the late forties, bush pilots had become more common in the area, and traffic to and from the south was increased. some trapping families earned enough that they could charter planes on to their hunting and trapping grounds rather than travelling by canoe. in the fifties and sixties, the government began to seriously work at 'opening up' the canadian north. roads and railways were built to the southern parts of cree territory; mining and logging companies began to exploit the resources in the region. increasingly, non-cree people moved to the region, with their own interests and concerns and with very little knowledge about what the cree thought or needed.

the cree took advantage of the opportunities created by these changes. many of them began to rely on summer jobs to add to their income from living off the land, especially after a drop in fur prices in the fifties. but there were less positive aspects to the new developments. cree hunters started to notice the effects of the resource development on the wildlife and the land. according to harvey feit, "hunters said animals became much less calm and less willing to be caught over large areas affected by noise generated by railways, road traffic, and airplanes now frequently traversing the region." (feit has a good article on the cree in the book, *native peoples: the canadian experience* edited by morrison and wilson.) they managed to convince the government to quit spraying pesticides along the roads, but also found that they were not being listened to or respected.

in 1965 a pulp and paper mill started up. this led to mercury pollution in many of the rivers and lakes. at the time, no one really knew about the effects of mercury, but, by the early seventies, the government had to warn the cree not to eat fish in much of the area because it might be contaminated. meanwhile, the government was building schools and nursing stations in the communities and encouraging the people to get full-time jobs and move away from life on the land. and the worst was yet to come. the government of quebec began to think on a huge scale about its own plan for intervening in the region.

clean green cheap power power power

in the spring of 1971, the government of quebec, under then premier robert bourassa, announced an ambitious plan to develop the hydroelectric potential of quebec's northern rivers. the james bay cree, whose traditional territory those rivers ran through, knew nothing about the plan until they heard it on the radio. they had not been consulted. thus began one of the major political struggles in canadian history, a struggle in which the government of quebec would learn the cost of ignoring the voices of the james bay cree. as anthropologist harvey feit has pointed out, the struggle was over power: who had power, what power was, how power could be generated, how different cultures thought of power, and empowerment.

the cree and inuit in the region began to meet and found they were almost unanimously opposed to the development. they decided to fight it. in the spring of

1972, they launched a court challenge in an attempt to stop the project. meanwhile, a government-appointed commission had been established to review quebec's claim to its northern territories. the dorion commission issued a report in 1972, acknowledging that aboriginal rights and titles were still held by the native people in northern quebec. however, the commission narrowly defined those rights in terms of hunting, fishing, and trapping.

the bourassa government responded to the dorion commission and the court challenge by announcing in october 1972 that the project would proceed. bourassa had pinned his hopes for improving quebec's economy on hydroelectric expansion, and said that the project was non-negotiable. the federal government, which had a trust-like responsibility towards the james bay cree, an obligation to act in their interest, as well as constitutional jurisdiction over "indians and lands reserved for indians," had taken the formal position of "alert neutrality." indian affairs minister jean chretien had, in essence, carefully decided to do nothing.

the cree and inuit proceeded with their court challenge. the court case was the longest hearing over the issue of a temporary injunction in canadian history. the cree were asking the court for a temporary injunction, which means a delay on construction, until their rights and titles could be determined. they brought their elders to court to talk about how they had always lived on the land. in november 1973, justice malouf handed down a very strong decision in favour of the cree and inuit. he ruled that the province was trespassing on traditional aboriginal territory and that aboriginal rights and titles had not been extinguished. he granted the injunction. one week later, the quebec court of appeal suspended the injunction and overturned malouf's decision after a one-day hearing. the supreme court of canada refused to listen to an appeal of that decision. even though it was overturned, malouf's decision had an important impact. it forced the government of quebec to begin negotiations with the james bay cree and inuit. those negotiations eventually led to a major land claim. there is a very good book about the james bay cree struggle, called *strangers devour the land* by boyce richardson. another good book about this struggle is roy macgregor's biography of billy diamond, called *chief.*

the james bay and northern quebec agreement

in november 1975, the james bay and northern quebec agreement was formally signed. this was the first modern land claim agreement. in some ways, it became the model for other land claims that would follow. the signatories to this claim were many. the government side included the government of quebec, hydro-quebec, the james bay project, and the government of canada. the aboriginal side included the northern quebec inuit association and the grand council of the crees of quebec.

the agreement was unusual in that the provincial government and the utility (hydro-quebec) took the lead from the government side. the federal government was actively involved but, unlike the case with later land claims, was not the leading party. interestingly, john ciaccia, who would later be the minister in charge of aboriginal affairs for the quebec government during the oka crisis, was a key government negotiator of the agreement.

it is important to emphasize that the james bay and northern quebec land claim was negotiated under a great deal of pressure. the quebec government agreed to negotiate in the first place only because of justice malouf's ruling that the province was trespassing on cree and inuit land. as well, the cree had the support of large sectors of the public, who, together with the cree, through demonstrations and protests, put a lot of pressure on the government to deal with aboriginal peoples.

as a result, this was not only the first but the fastest land claim negotiation. the whole deal was basically negotiated in just over a year. some of the problems that emerged later can be traced to the fact that the deal was so rushed. overall, the deal involved a payment of $232 million over twenty-one years to the aboriginal peoples in the james bay region. only $32 million of that was to be paid by the federal government. the aboriginal people got 5,500 square kilometres of land for their exclusive use. they also got exclusive hunting, fishing, and trapping rights over another sixty thousand square kilometres of land, which were to be jointly managed with the government.

the deal included an income security program for aboriginal hunters and trappers. profits from the hydroelectric dams were used to ensure that aboriginal peoples living off the land had a stable annual income. as well, the deal involved some changes to the hydro project, provisions for local government, and the setting up of native-controlled health and education boards. in exchange for these benefits, the cree and inuit of the james bay region agreed to "cede, release, surrender and convey all their native claims, rights, titles and interests" to their traditional territories. that meant that the quebec government could proceed with construction of the roads and dams that were part of the james bay hydroelectric project. the deal was controversial from the start. many activists inside and outside the cree community accused the leadership of selling out. others said that the deal was the best the cree could hope for.

what a surprise: new treaties are treated the same way old treaties were treated!

the james bay and northern quebec agreement was settled in 1975. in january of 1978, an amendment to the agreement was made, called the northeastern quebec agreement, adding the naskapi. by the late seventies, the quebec government had passed twenty pieces of legislation relating to the land claim agreement. however, serious problems had developed in the implementation of the land claim. these problems were in the areas of health, social services, economic development, and social development.

both sides felt they had a mutual understanding of how things would work, but lawyers for the government side began to undermine these understandings. the cree found that the government would not live up to a commitment unless it was very clearly specified in the agreement. in an article on land claims in alberta and quebec (found in a book called *governments in conflict?*), james o'rielly argued that "where the obligations and commitments in the agreement depended on understandings reached during negotiations or on the good faith of the government of quebec, the province refused to implement the provisions of the agreement." the cree complained to the federal government, which conducted a review. they promised some changes and additional funding. in 1984 self-government legislation was passed, called the *cree-naskapi act*, which replaced aspects of the *indian act*. bands began to act as local governments and owners of cree lands.

meanwhile, the people found that the flooding from the dams had devastated their territory. the mercury released into the water made it very difficult for people to practise their traditional ways, even with the income supplement program established in the land claim. in the early 1990s, faced with plans for phase two of the james bay hydro-development project, matthew coon-come, grand chief of the crees of quebec, said that the land claim agreement was not working. the cree were prepared to tear it up. the struggle over the future of this region and its first nations continues.

there is a book of poetry called *james bay memoirs* by margaret sam-cromarty, which provides a personal view of some of the events of the last few decades. i will close with a few lines from a poem called "ballad of a river": "the happy river was lost / it weeps now. / it seeks / golden sands. / the chisasibi river - / its soul calling / hears the old people / no more."

white upon white

on june 25, 1969, jean chretien announced a new policy on indian affairs to the house of commons. this now infamous 'white paper' triggered an extraordinary struggle between aboriginal and government leaders. in order to understand the struggle, we need to know a bit about the policy itself.

the policy was based on the belief that all the problems of aboriginal peoples stemmed from one basic source: discrimination. if you could end discrimination, you could end the problems. this view agreed with then prime minister trudeau's personal philosophy, which was individualistic and rationalist. the other basis of the policy was the idea that something dramatic had to be done. indian affairs could not continue to stagnate. this would not be a policy of half measures. the white paper proposed six broad policy objectives and then five immediate steps that could be taken to meet the goals. the objectives were:

1. to remove any legal basis for discrimination of indians;
2. to recognize the positive contribution of indian culture to canadian society;
3. to provide services to all canadians, including indians, through the same channels;
4. to help those furthest behind the most;

5. to recognize any legal obligations towards indians; and
6. to transfer control of indian lands to indian people.

these goals were to be achieved through the following steps, which were to be taken immediately after the policy was adopted:

1. repeal the *indian act* and turn over title of lands to indians;
2. transfer responsibility for indians to the provinces;
3. provide funding for economic development;
4. dissolve the indian affairs branch; and
5. appoint a commissioner to develop procedures for deciding how to deal with land claims.

trudeau was quite clear about what this would mean in the long run, even for treaty rights. in a speech in vancouver on august 8, 1969, he said: "it's inconceivable i think that in a given society, one section of the society have a treaty with the other section of the society. we must all be equal under the laws and we must not sign treaties amongst ourselves and many of those treaties indeed would have less and less significance in the future anyhow." he went on to say, "we can't recognize aboriginal rights because no society can be built on historical 'might-have-beens.'" although it was not specifically mentioned in the policy proposals themselves, trudeau's comments meant that people also associated the white paper with the idea that treaties should be ended.

in proposing to end discrimination against indians, the policy was trying to do something positive for indians. however, much of the discrimination it proposed to end amounted to what could be called 'positive discrimination' or what today we would call 'aboriginal rights.' this is why the policy was soon under attack from most aboriginal leaders.

fight the paper!

the struggle over the white paper shaped a generation of aboriginal political activists and had a very important influence on government policy in the years that followed. when indian affairs minister jean chretien announced the white paper, he implied that it had included consultations with indian leaders. while chretien had met with many indian leaders prior to the announcement, he had not provided them with details about the policy. the government had indeed engaged in extensive consultations with first nations communities prior to drafting the white paper. the problem was, they almost entirely ignored what they heard.

after chretien's speech, aboriginal leaders felt a growing sense of shock as they realized what the impact of the policy would be. the president of the manitoba indian brotherhood, david courchene, said, "the shock hit us all and it hit us in the gallery [of the house of commons]. we had no preview." they quickly decided to fight the policy. criticism of the policy as assimilationist and racist began to grow, led by the indian association of alberta under then president harold cardinal. cardinal wrote that the policy meant "the only good indian is a non-indian." initially, it was the provincial and territorial level organizations that took the lead in attacking the white paper, with the national indian brotherhood still going through growing pains.

the government stood firmly behind the policy at first, but, by the fall of 1969, it grew more defensive, with chretien and trudeau saying that the white paper was only a proposal for discussion. however, when, that december, they appointed dr. lloyd barber as land claims commissioner in line with a white paper proposal, reaction was intense and angry. his office was boycotted. eventually, barber got his mandate expanded beyond its original scope and came to be seen by many aboriginal leaders as someone with whom they could work.

one aboriginal leader, william wuttunee, who had led the native indian council in the early sixties (a mostly cultural organization that got government funding and sponsored events such as "indian princess" pageants!), was hired by the government in early 1970 to promote the white paper. wuttunee's band almost had him banned from his own reserve, and, by spring of the same year, he resigned. the government by then was coming under more criticism as academics and journalists began to side with the native organizations. by the spring of 1970, trudeau was saying, "we're not going to force [the white paper] down their throats," but aboriginal leaders were still concerned that it was official policy, and kept the pressure on.

the national indian brotherhood, under a new leader, george manuel, began to take a primary role in the struggle against the white paper. the intensity of the anger of aboriginal leaders, which was heavily reported by the media, caught the government by surprise. the anger grew as the government seemed to be sticking with the policy. in early june of 1970, indian leaders had a meeting at carleton university, sponsored by the nib, where they adopted a slightly modified version of the red paper, which had been written by harold cardinal and proposed by the indian association of alberta. they proposed a profoundly different set of policies based on respect for aboriginal and treaty rights.

a hasty meeting was arranged with the federal cabinet on june 4, and the red paper was ceremonially presented. trudeau made an off-the-cuff speech that indicated victory for the aboriginal leaders. however, it was not until march 17, 1971, when, in a speech called "the unfinished tapestry - indian policy in canada," chretien formally withdrew the white paper, that indian leaders knew the white paper was not going to be the official government policy. in spite of this, many aboriginal leaders felt that the white paper continued to be a 'hidden agenda' of the government. two books by aboriginal participants on opposite sides of the struggle provide material on the white paper. they are william wuttunee's *ruffled feathers* and harold cardinal's *the unjust society.*

new times or old patterns

in indian country, the sixties was a time when sea changes led to crises and conflict, and ultimately to a new paradigm in indian-government relations. the changes that had been made to the *indian act* in 1951, while leaving much of the colonial mechanisms in place, had removed the worst restrictions on status indians. importantly, they were free to move from reserves without needing indian agent permission and this, with other demographic changes like a rising population, growing unemployment, poor services and opportunites on reserves, led to a substantial migration to urban areas. the perceived 'indian problem' in canada became a more visible one. at the same time, aboriginal political activists of earlier decades – fred loft, andrew paull, malcolm norris, john tootoosis, jules sioui – had laid the groundwork for a new generation of dissident political leaders prepared to take a more confrontational approach with government.

in the period since, government has not been able to write any old policy it wanted. aboriginal peoples, by ensuring constitutional recognition of their rights, arguably prevented any policy framework like the white paper, premised on the eradication of aboriginal rights, from ever again being developed. yet, still, somehow, this remains the aim of a far-right-wing, but influential, rump of the new conservative party.

in this era, we have seen the words "the existing aboriginal and treaty rights of the aboriginal peoples of canada are hereby recognized and affirmed" placed in the constitution (s 35). we have seen a royal commission on aboriginal peoples led by aboriginal peoples. we have seen a florescence of indigenous artists, writers, politicians, filmmakers, athletes, academics, jurists, architects, and leaders in all areas of activity. and yet, there are those continuing to promote "economic development," modernization, progress, relocation of communities, and the continuation of the colonial conquest under the guise of these terms. new struggles – oka, stoney point, grassy narrows – and continuations of old struggles – hydro development in northern manitoba, in northern quebec, a new mackenzie gas project – also have emerged. the spirit of resistence remains strong not only in people like elizabeth penashue, judy dasilva, kahntineta horn, herb norwegian, and so many others, but in communities that deserve the name "community."

in northern manitoba, a single community, once known as the cross lake first nation, decides it will not sign an agreement extinguishing the rights it won in the seventies through a modern treaty called the northern flood agreement. it passes a 'first written law' and forms a new structure based on four councils. it refuses to co-operate with the further ravaging of its great river. it stands its ground. there is still courage in the real world. there are still those who believe in something other than unbridled greed as a principle of life. many of them, around the world and in canada's backyard, are indigenous. their history of the modern era will look very different from the stories of progress told as self-satisfied idle chat at the dining tables of the greedy and powerful.

endnote

i thank lee selleck for his work in encouraging the original versions of these pieces; i treasure our friendship, crossing as it does vast chasms of time and space. i am also very grateful to peter ives and his arbeiter ring colleagues for the intelligence and caring they gave in guiding this text to completion; to pat sanders for her patient and diligent and careful, yet creative, copy editing; and to jarvis robin brownlie for a series of thoughtful and helpful corrective comments in reviewing a late draft of this work.

i thank my daughter, the impossibly sweet and inspiringly beautiful malay, for every precious moment of love, laughter and life she gifts me. etched in my heart beside her name sits yours, jaime drew.

i offer these words in this way at this time to honour the memories of jamie tudor, jim evoy, tom jewiss, philip robinson and david brophy. in the too short span of time they had, each in his own way cast a light on how newcomers can live in a truly respectful way with aboriginal peoples.